THE LOVE SPHERE OF THE EARTH

The Love Sphere of the Earth

AWAKENING THE NUCLEAR POWER OF THE HUMAN HEART

Marko Pogačnik

Lindisfarne Books
2025

Published by Lindisfarne Books
an imprint of SteinerBooks/Anthroposophic Press, Inc.
834 Route 203, Spencertown, NY 12165
www.steinerbooks.org

Illustrations by Marko Pogačnik
Front cover cosmogram by Marko Pogačnik

ISBN 978-1-58420-877-8 (paperback)

Printed in the United States of America

Contents

Motto

Observe and listen
around you,
with your heart.
Allow yourself
a new discovery,
in harmony with me,
beloved human being.

Message from Gaia

(received through Andrea Rosslan-Brandt)

Introduction

In the face of a war against all life on the Earth, including human life – a war that constantly puts on shifting masks – I have been granted the vision, in part through dreams, of an extensive heart and love system on Earth.

At the end of January 2022, just before the worldwide pandemic turned into a merciless war, I began to describe the love sphere of the Earth and the love fields pulsating between its beings. When I then turned to the love potentialities of human beings, I discovered – with joyful surprise – what wondrous treasures the human being carries within that can contribute to the peace and beauty of life on Earth.

I describe these treasures of love now so that everyone can become aware of them. And, to this end, I have also developed exercises that can help to awaken the heart's potentialities.

With this book, I wish to strengthen the hope that the newly awakened core power of the human heart will enable us to collectively accumulate enough love potency to overcome the threatening circumstances of our times.

Marko Pogačnik, Šempas, March 11, 2022

1
The transformation of the Earth and the human being is in full swing

Having crossed the threshold into the third millennium of our era, the human family is encountering a difficult bottleneck. On the one hand, we are victims of a civilization that follows the logic of the mechanistic mind, which threatens to transform us into cybernetic servants of our own concepts. And on the other hand, we feel powerless in the face of so-called climate change that could destroy the Earth's living conditions and life systems. What is actually happening to our home planet and what is the role of our tirelessly beating heart that stands as a symbol for all-connecting love?

Before we go into more detail about the core power of the human heart, I would like to talk briefly about my experiences of the current processes of Planet Earth. For the past twenty years, I have been talking about the Earth's transformation process, always in an optimistic way, as a counterbalance to climate change.

I use the term "Earth transformation" to refer to a partly invisible process whose phenomena I have been observing since late autumn 1997. This transformation is about the Earth as a planet imbued with elemental consciousness that is gradually and imperceptibly but consciously changing its manifestation in the subtle areas of its planetary body. This creates a multidimensional Earth realm that does not erase the existence of the three-dimensional reality with which we are familiar but incorporates it into a new, broader-dimensional composition.

This new interdimensional composition is a fabric woven out of different realities: the visible material as well as the invisible vital-energetic, elemental and spiritual dimensions. I have been privileged to observe this phenomenon in the many workshops I have conducted in natural and urban landscapes that have focused on the perception of the subtle levels of nature and the transformational processes of the Earth.

Our home planet is undergoing a transformation

We can assume that developments in the cosmos obey a cyclical principle. In order for something new to emerge – in our case a multidimensional Earth body – there must be a clearing away of what inhibits development. So-called climate change represents the shadow side of the Earth transformation process. But we should not attribute this process solely to the activity and wisdom of the Earth. In a hindering, negative way, not-yet awakened human beings are continuously projecting their limited mental images onto the Earth body, denying the multidimensionality that has existed since time immemorial. Imagine the consequences of millions, of billions, of human beings consistently imagining and projecting an image of the Earth as an exclusively materialized sphere.

On Good Friday before Easter of 2021, I received the following dream illustrating the tragedy of such a tightly sealed Earth image:

I see a giant holding the Earth, which I recognize as it is often described by astronauts – a beautiful sphere adorned with life. The giant grasps the globe with both hands, and then I notice that it is actually a concrete sphere painted with oil colors. He lifts the sphere up high and throws it to the ground. It breaks into thousands of fragments, each of which simultaneously takes on a beautifully rounded spherical shape.

A second dream followed on the same night:

I am one of a group of eighth-grade students whom I am observing in my dream. We are out in nature and have to complete certain tasks in a competition. I am kneeling in front of a flat stone that is set upright in the ground with a rectangular opening carved into it. The task is to put my head through the opening. Previously I was able to do the task easily, but this time I find that the opening is too narrow. Despite repeated attempts, I do not succeed. I am irritated. I want to get my stone masonry tools to widen the opening. I ask the teacher if putting my head through the stone opening is compulsory.

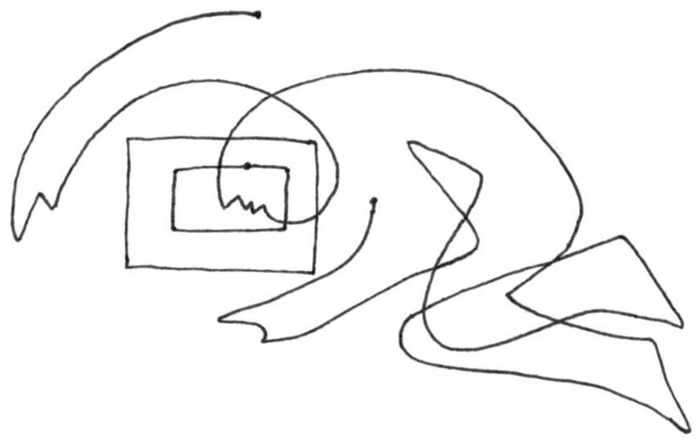

Due to an increased level of vibration, my head no longer fits through the opening in the stone

The two dreams taken together address the present Earth transformation process. The first dream with the Earth as a painted concrete sphere lets us know that the planet is so densely surrounded by human concepts, power patterns, and settlement projects that its aliveness has no chance of lasting for the long term. This is why Earth's creator and goddess, Gaia (from the Greek), has set in motion certain processes of dismantling and transformation in order to make way for the renewal of the multidimensional quality of the Earth.

The dream of the stone with the narrow opening refers to the complementary process that takes place, or should take place, within the human being. This is the renewal of human sensitivity, the further development of which, however, is inhibited by our predominating mental concepts – symbolized in the dream by my oversized head. In order to perceive the phenomena of Earth transformation and to keep up with the changes, we must first awaken our finer organs of feeling to develop loving relationships with the elemental and spiritual realms of the earthly universe.

The tragedy of the Earth transformation is that whereas human beings are constantly inundated with the harrowing news of climate change, they are not aware of the uplifting and joyful processes of Earth transformation that are simultaneously in full swing. These are taking place on the subtle levels of the Earth, but there is little opportunity today for human beings to train their sensitivity in order to experience and understand these subtle levels of reality and integrate them into their own worldview. Such a training should be taught as a main subject in every primary school!

The hijacking of our capacity to love

We can succeed in activating the incredible transformational potentialities of love only if we first clear away certain hurdles that obscure access to the new expansion of the human heart system. A dream that I recently received can help us recognize the basis of these hurdles.

I am sitting in a relatively small, rounded space. I am able only to sit bent over in it. I feel the inner urge to tidy it up, but when I look around, I see that there is nothing to do. The room looks completely empty, except for a few dried-up tree leaves on the floor. When I turn my gaze upwards, I see my own head above my ribcage in a brilliant white light that radiates like the Sun. In the glaring light, my head seems to shine even more strongly than the Sun.

The space that I am occupying in the dream I can immediately recognize as my own chest. The pronounced contrast between the apparent emptiness of the ribcage, the ancestral space of the heart, and the obvious supremacy of the head, the seat of the mind, is obvious here. Without pondering too much about the dream image, we can understand the symbolism as referring to the relationship between the logic of the modern mind and the logic of the heart's feelings. In this dream image, the mind seems to be far more potent than the heart—but is that all there is to it? As you certainly have experienced, dream images are often accompanied by feelings. In this case, when I saw the radiant head, I had the clear feeling that this was a deliberate theft of power on the part of the mind. According to the dream, the heart beating in the chest has become the victim of this robbery.

My head shines in the light, but my heart space is empty

I received this dream exactly two years after the so-called Covid-19 pandemic had started its devastating march through the human family—and shortly before I myself was to suffer the Covid disease. It is well known that this disease takes over the heart-chest area, and subsequently many patients cannot manage without the intervention of artificial respiration.

One conclusion could be that one of the objectives of the Covid pandemic is to rob human beings of their capacity to love in order to inflate the power of the intellect exponentially. What purpose could be served by the mind acquiring exaggerated domination over the power of the heart's love? How might we imagine the hijacking of the capacity for love in modern human beings? The answer to this question can be found in the second dream I was given shortly before I fell ill.

Since time immemorial, the ability of our consciousness to ascend from the everyday level to a higher level has been represented by the symbol of a ladder. On this higher level, the human being feels included in the wholeness and community of all living things. In my opinion, this is also where the love relationships on Earth and in the universe converge. In the Bible, this ladder is called "Jacob's Ladder" because in the vision of the prophet Jacob, angels descend from heaven to Earth and ascend again. I have made it a habit to climb a ladder when I want to tune in wholistically. In my dream, however, I can't find the ladder.

Irritated, I walk around the house and call out quite loudly for my mother to ask her for the ladder. But she is not to be found and does not hear me calling. Eventually, instead of the usual ladder, I discover a new means of climbing that looks technically sophisticated. It is made of taut ropes with, seemingly useless, wheels. Seeing no other way to get up, I decide to use the means available, but as I begin to climb my body starts to sway dangerously because all of my weight is swinging on the ropes. There is not the possibility of a firm grip here, as I am used to with conventional ladders.

It is only with great difficulty that I reach my desired level of consciousness. Other people are already present, but I am separated from them by a wide wall resembling a curtain of several layers with thin steel rings from which hang bags filled with goods from the supermarket. It takes all my strength to fight my way through these bags. Finally, I reach the group of people on the other side and am amazed to see that they are relaxing on cloud-like beanbags, listening to a teacher whom I don't know give a speech that is full of well-worn, conventional "wisdom". Indignantly, I straighten up and say in a loud voice: "We are ready to dedicate ourselves to our common tasks now!" But no one listens to me. It is as if I am not even present.

Putting the two dreams together, I hear the message that as humanity on the threshold of the third millennium, we are confronted with the attempt to silence our heart's potentialities, perhaps even to switch them off as a source of love and replace them with an oversized megamind. Gaia, creator of the earthly cosmos, has granted us access to a higher level of consciousness anchored in human memory, so that we can develop creative and loving relationships with each other and with our companion world. The dream with the ladder explains how access to this level can be blocked through intimidating measures, such as those introduced in response to the dangers of the pandemic.

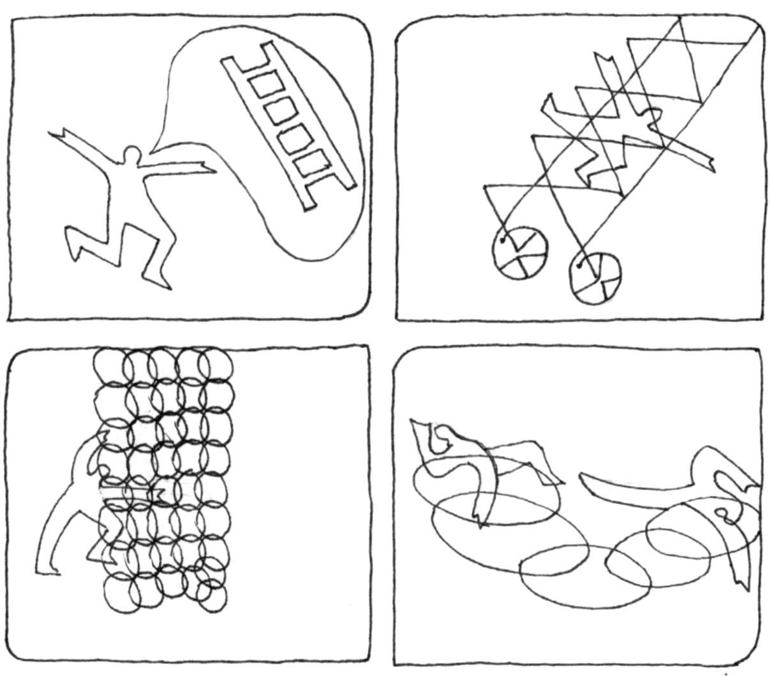

My dream with the false ladder

But using threats has never proven to be a means of healing interpersonal relationships. Another negative strategy may be to tinker with certain ascension techniques that are meant to raise the human mind to a level that seems to surpass the power of the heart through its strong, mentally generated light. We should be aware, however, that this strong light is neither grounded nor connected to the cosmic sources and cannot, therefore, have any influence on the further development of the human being and Planet Earth.

The tragedy of the lack of heart-based interpersonal and social relationships is represented in the dream by the wide wall, the curtain with the bags of supermarket goods. As we climb along the new ladder-like structure to the seemingly "higher" level of consciousness, we end up in a chaotic overabundance of items that can in no way satisfy the human being's thirst for truth, love, and freedom. The last sequence of the dream leads us to the realization that, despite the super-modern faculties that lead to the supposedly higher level of human development, we are in fact being catapulted back to an already outdated level of egocentric existence. There is no trace of creative power and enthusiasm here, or the will to perceive our relationships with the Earth and its visible as well as invisible entities on a deeper level, so that a new loving community between Earth, human beings, and cosmos can be founded.

This shall be enough said about the shadow side that wants to keep us from fully dedicating ourselves to the multidimensional heart system of the Earth and human beings. As a transition to the luminous and hopeful side, I will now present my interpretation of Grimm's fairy tale of "Rapunzel" that describes the sequential phases of the love process.

2
A story of the unfolding of love

Grimm's fairy tale of "Rapunzel"

Fairy tales have been passed down through oral tradition over centuries and have been shaped by the cultural ideas of many peoples. Through their pictorial language, they can convey our human motives and the forces at work when we seek access to the lost expanses of the earthly cosmos. They may also contain a subterranean stream of knowledge that was considered heretical and suppressed by the prevailing cultural rules or religious dogmas of their time. This is true of the fairy tales of the Brothers Grimm, whose stories were written on the threshold of modern times and have been handed down in the vernacular for centuries. I rediscovered these tales not long ago when I was writing a book in Slovenian entitled *Grimm's Fairy Tales for Adults*. In the tale of "Rapunzel" I found archetypes that show the different phases of the love process. Here is the tale as I adapted it from Grimm's "Rapunzel".

Phase One: Falling in love

> *Once upon a time there were a woman and a man who had long wished in vain for a child. Unexpectedly, they had reason to hope that their wish might come true. The back of their house had a small window overlooking the neighbor's magnificent garden, full of the most beautiful flowers, herbs, and vegetables. It was, however, surrounded by a high wall and no one dared to enter because it belonged to an enchantress who had extraordinary powers. She was feared by the whole world.*

I want to emphasize here that the garden is located at the back of the house, and we can only see it through a small window. Assuming this fairy tale unveils a secret of the human being, the small window could symbolize the connection with the space located behind the human back. With our eyes we can see only the embodied world in front of us, thus the space behind our back stands for the invisible dimensions of the Earth, the universe, and humanity. So here we are talking about the causal [primordial] world where, on an energetic level, archetypes and also prototypes exist that determine the way the common or physical world is shaped and the way it functions.

The magical garden is a good symbol of this causal dimension: the beds of vegetables, herbs, and flowers can be understood as individual master patterns or matrices in which certain values and forces are anchored and ordered. In the next phase of evolution, they will have a decisive influence on the nature and orientation of the world in which we live.

One day the woman was standing at her window, looking down into the magical garden, and there she saw a bed planted with the most beautiful rampions (rapunzel). And they looked so fresh and green that she felt an irresistible desire to eat some. Because she knew that they were unattainable, her craving increased every day – she was completely overcome by it. She became paler and paler and more and more exhausted.

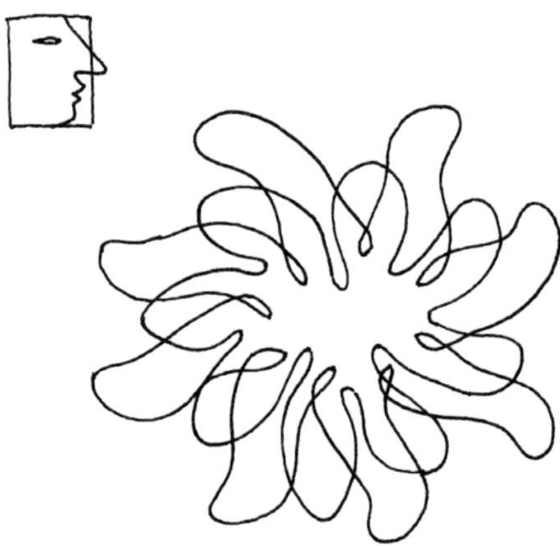

The view through the window at the back of the body

The woman's craving at the sight of the green rampions shows us how the causal background of the embodied world is revealing to her a primordial pattern or matrix of something that is mostly missing in the human world – something that every human being wants to experience or embody; hence, the woman's inevitable desire to taste it.

Can the natural appearance, shape, and color of the rampion tell us something about this discovered archetype? Rampion is one of the few varieties of lettuce that grows freely in nature, and it is extremely tasty. When I was a little boy, once a week a slight old woman came to our house to sell my mother a small bowl of rampions she had gathered in the fields. The rampion has the shape of a rosette with leaves dancing around a core. It resembles the representations of the chakras, the vital-energetic centers of the human body from the Indian yoga tradition. Its lush green color can certainly be seen to symbolize the heart center, which is normally perceived as green.

Then her husband was frightened and asked: "What ails you, dear wife?"

"Oh!" she replied. "If I cannot eat some of the rampions from the garden behind our house, I will die."

This first part of the fairy tale reveals that the vibrating presence of love is a primordial force on the causal level of the universe – an essence preceding love's appearance in the manifest life. Love is, first of all, a cosmic matrix impervious to the agency of the human will, bestowed upon us through a process that cannot be controlled by our conscious mind. In this way, love resembles the inspiration of artistic creation. Anyone who has ever fallen madly in love knows that love strikes us like the arrow of Eros, and we are unable to avoid it. We can see from the woman's irresistible desire for the rampions that she would rather die than live without the manifest inspiration of love in her life.

Fearing his wife might die, the man decides to climb over the high wall during the night and bring her a handful of rampions.

But after she has tasted of the elemental power of love, her desire for the sweet vibration becomes all the stronger, and the man has to climb over the fence again the next night. But this time he is caught by the enchantress who guards the causal plane of the life processes.

First of all, we should free the enchantress (she is a sorceress or witch in some versions of the fairy tale) from the curse attached to this designation. The word derives from words like "enchanting" and "enchantment" (also in the sense of magic) which in themselves do not contain any negative connotation. They not only denote human creativity, but also express an activity of other beings that goes beyond the logically perceptible and explainable.

From this perspective, the enchantress of the magic garden can be seen as the guardian of the causal world and its archetypes and forces. Where human beings are allowed unhindered access to the causal world in their search for scientific knowledge, they may damage the physical world and its beings through irresponsible and unconscious actions. Unfortunately, these limits are already being transgressed and violated by the manipulation of human DNA, the misuse of nuclear power, the genetic manipulation of plants, and the like.

In the enchantress I recognize Gaia, the creator and preserver of Earth's universe, who reveals herself as a wise teacher of humanity. She knows the way to the power of the heart. As the story progresses, she leads people from one station to the next on the path of human knowledge, so that they may discover their own heart powers and heart qualities.

The enchantress allows the man to take as much of the rampion as he wants, but only on the condition that he brings her the child his wife will give birth to. Fearing the enchantress, the man promises to fulfill her demands. Soon afterwards, his wife gives birth to a girl. Immediately after the birth, the enchantress appears, gives the child the name "Rapunzel" [another name for rampion], and takes the child away.

Phase Two: The internalization of the love quality

Rapunzel becomes the most beautiful child under the Sun. When she reaches twelve years of age, the enchantress takes her to a remote forest and locks her in a tower that has neither stairs nor a door and only a small window at the top. Now, Rapunzel's long magnificent hair is as fine as spun gold. Whenever the enchantress wanted to enter the tower, she stood at the bottom and called out: "Rapunzel, Rapunzel, let down your hair". When Rapunzel heard the enchantress's voice, she untied her golden braid, wrapped it around the window hook at the top, and let it fall down twenty cubits so that the enchantress could climb up.

As already indicated, this fairy tale acquaints us with the various aspects of the human relationship to the power of love and its all-encompassing values. In the first phase, love is experienced as an inspiration from the causal level of the cosmos. In the lonely tower we reach the second stage on the human journey to the secrets of our own heart system. Rapunzel is initiated into the secrets of the heart not from her mother—that is, not in the environment of the human family—but from the enchantress, Gaia. The lonely tower in the middle of the forest marks a station on the way to the heart where the Earth, personified by Gaia herself, with her elemental consciousness appears as the teacher of the laws of love. The school of the heart is now at the elemental level of the natural environment. It is symbolically connected to the golden braid, which for me represents the human spine, a channel of the forces of life and love. Symbolically, each time the enchantress climbs up the golden braid to the window of the heart, the elemental love from the treasury of the Earth's heart ascends via our spine to our human hearts, and from there inspires our love for the whole world of existence.

Unfortunately, people today have almost completely forgotten about their relationship with the love and wisdom of the elemental dimensions of the Earth. Therefore, the power of human love is not strong enough to overcome egoism and self-centeredness in both secular and spiritual terms. Love may flow within the narrow circle of one's own family, religious, and ethnic communities, but other fellow human beings or beings of other species who do not meet these criteria may not receive love, but quite the opposite in the form of hostility or even hatred. The primal force of love does exist in the human being but is experienced first and foremost as an inner process.

Phase Three: The love relationship

After a few years, the king's son was riding through the forest and noticed the mysterious tower. Then he heard a song floating out from the high window. It was so sweet that he stopped and listened. It was Rapunzel passing the time in her loneliness by singing. The king's son wanted to climb up to her and looked for a door in the tower, but there was none to be found. He rode home, but the singing had so deeply touched his heart that he went out into the forest every day to listen.

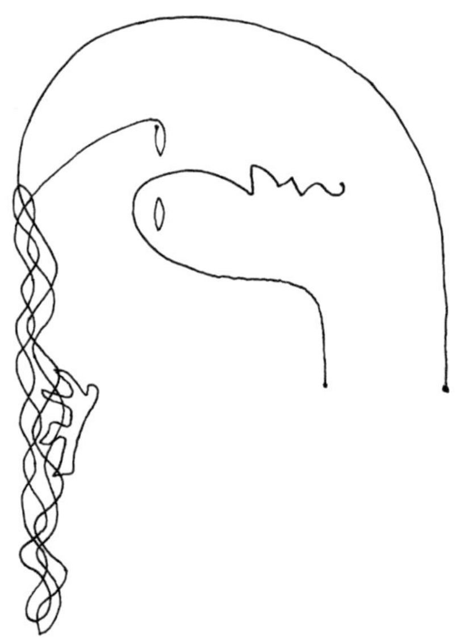

Love can overcome all obstacles

Once, as the prince was standing behind a tree, he saw the enchantress approaching and heard her call up: "Rapunzel, Rapunzel, let down your hair". Thereby he discovered the solution to the secret as to how he could ascend to the singer in the tower. He repeated the enchantress's call, and the next moment the braid came down and he climbed up.

At first Rapunzel was terrified, but eventually they became friends, and then they fell in love and they decided they would get married. Rapunzel and the king's son agreed that he would visit her every evening and bring a strand of silk each time so that Rapunzel could weave a ladder from it to finally climb down from the tower to solid ground herself.

It should be pointed out that a king, a prince, or a queen in a Grimm's fairy tale usually represents the dimensions that can be called "cosmic". By this I do not mean necessarily outer space, but I am thinking of dimensions that go beyond any human ability to perceive them – they are all-embracing. The encounter between Rapunzel as the adopted daughter of Gaia and the prince is about an encounter and connection between love as an elemental power and love as a cosmic force that flows forever through all of creation.

At this level of consciousness of the true values of the heart, we are beginning to connect the elemental power of love in the human being with the angelic dimension of the heart, which has the strength to keep the whole universe in harmonious movement and creativity. In the story of Rapunzel, a woman and a man experience themselves as representatives of the two sources of love, and they plan their joint descent to Earth as equal partners.

However, the embodiment of their already existing relationship – which is living together on the physical level of reality – is yet to come, hence their plan for a silken ladder.

For now, their relationship is still secret, which means that it takes place as an inner process. Rapunzel becomes pregnant, but how can she bear the child she is expecting in a tower to which there is no door and without the helping hands that motherhood requires?

Phase Four: Walking through the transformation process

And so, they were happy and joyful for some time. The enchantress did not find out, until one day Rapunzel said to her: "Tell me, dear lady, how it happens that my little dresses are getting so tight and don't want to fit anymore?"

"Oh, you godless child," said the sorceress, "what must I hear from you!"

In her anger, the enchantress grabbed Rapunzel's golden hair. She whipped it around her left hand once, twice, grabbed a pair of scissors with her right, and rip, rip, she cut it off. Rapunzel's beautiful tresses lay on the ground. Then she took poor Rapunzel to a lonely hut in the middle of the forest, where she had to live in great misery and discomfort.

On the same day that she had cast Rapunzel out, that evening the enchantress fastened the cut tresses to the top of the window hook, and when the king's son came and called out, "Rapunzel, Rapunzel, let down your hair," she let down the golden braid.

The king's son climbed up, but he did not find his dearest Rapunzel at the top, but the enchantress, who looked at him with such a poisonous gaze that in his despair he threw himself from the tower into the depths. The thorns into which he fell pierced his eyes so that he wandered blindly in the forest, eating nothing but roots and berries, and doing nothing but wailing and weeping over the loss of his dearest lady.

It seems as if Rapunzel and the king's son became victims of an evil and merciless sorceress. In reality, however, they are facing the often painful process of transformation that human beings who are living in a culture with a mainly superficial idea of love have to go through if they want to embody the true value and power of love in everyday life. This is indeed not an easy task, because it is about incarnating the value of love in all its greatness and depth. Rapunzel and the king's son bonded in such love when they met in the lonely tower high above the ground of everyday life. However, to bring the same power and beauty of love to the ground and at once live it in the practical world is a challenging hurdle.

This part of the fairy tale is reminiscent of the biblical story of the expulsion of Adam and Eve from Paradise. In the past, the Earth in the form of the enchantress ensured that human beings received everything they needed to survive and sustain their community. But now Rapunzel, the female aspect of humanity, has to work hard in solitude to feed the twin children she has since given birth to.

The king's son, the male aspect of humanity, like Adam expelled from Paradise, represents a psychological condition that is often treated in the Grimm's fairy tales as the curse of our age: he becomes blind to the feelings of the heart as a result of his rational view of life. Thus, the king's son cannot recall his true origins and the meaning of his existence in the sphere of the Earth.

Phase Five: The love relationship becomes grounded

After wandering around for years, one day the king's son finally comes near the lonely cottage where Rapunzel lives with the twins she has given birth to, a boy and a girl. The king's son hears a voice, and it seems so familiar to him that he goes towards it. Rapunzel recognizes him and embraces him, crying. Two of her tears fall on his eyes. They are healed, and he can see as before. He brings his family home to his kingdom, where they are received with joy and live happily ever after.

The conclusion of the fairy tale seems to be rounded off with a "happy ending," but there is more to know here. There are two important moments that I would like to draw attention to. One is that it is the sound of Rapunzel's voice that helps the wandering, blinded prince to find the direction to his beloved and to his true home. It is the voice of the original love resounding in our hearts that we should listen to, so we can always find a meaningful direction in life. Secondly, I think of Rapunzel's two tears falling on the prince's unseeing eyes and restoring his sight. Here attention is drawn to the healing and creative power of the element of water when it is imbued with the qualities of mercy, love, and joy. Water is honored as a medium through which love is made possible. Thanks to it we can be creative in everyday life, above and beyond what the human mind thinks possible.

3
The way that trees and stones love

Before we can grant love its full space as a cosmic force and the matrix of consciousness, we have to let go of some cherished beliefs, such as that love is an exclusively human affair. To this end, I would like to share with you some of my experiences of love relationships in nature.

When I conducted a workshop in Berlin-Zehlendorf in the autumn of 2021, our workshop group visited Messel Park, where Rudolf Steiner House is located. In the park there is a beech grove that I thought was suitable for gaining experience of how individual trees lovingly connect with each other in community. Very deliberately I use the term "lovingly" here because our interest is in a specific level of relationships in nature called, in the faery language, "Anwa".

I have adopted the term Anwa from my friend David Spangler, whom I met in the early 1970s, when I first visited the ecologically and spiritually oriented Findhorn community in Scotland, and with whom I have carried out many joint projects and workshops over the years. A few years ago, he published two books in which he recorded his conversations with a Sidhe woman called Mariel. In the second book, *Engaging with the Sidhe,* the term Anwa plays an essential role. The faery folk of the Sidhe (pronunciation of this Celtic word is "She") inhabit a spherical space that exists parallel to our physical Earth as an aspect of the Earth universe. This faery people is not embodied in matter but lives and weaves as a hologram in etheric space. More on this can be found in my books *Dancing with the Earth Changes* and *Creating Gaia Culture.*

Loving relationships imbued with the quality of Anwa are the first to nullify the distance between subject and object that is assumed by some aspects of natural science because, as quantum physics well knows, the observer as subject influences the object of observation. Be aware that the tree you are looking at is also, in its own way, "looking at you" and exploring your micro-universe. Trees are curious beings. The mutual perception happens on a higher level of consciousness and can certainly be called a dialogue. However, since the entities of nature, unlike humans, do not have access to a mental level of consciousness, this dialogue is more like a love relationship – of course, this can happen only if the person involved is open to it.

But Anwa means even more. It is not only about the individual relationship between two subjects, such as a tree and a rock or a human being and a river. In a relationship in the spirit of Anwa, ambience also plays a role in the exchange between entities. Thus, the constellation of stars at any given moment as well as the elemental and spiritual guardians of the place can participate in this common dance too. During encounters in the shared space of Anwa, transformations of human and more-than-human beings occur, because each time new insights into the secrets of creation are granted.

The situation is quite different in our culture, permeated as it is with intellectual patterns. When people come into contact with nature, those who assume that trees and stones have no consciousness and no heart dimension may close themselves off from the elemental eros of nature. Instead, a diffuse feeling may rise up in them, as if the entities of nature and the landscape desire to invade the space of their heart, and they feel threatened and frightened. Furthermore, there are cultural habits and patterns that lead us to see everything around us as objects separate from ourselves. Thus, paradoxically, people may claim that they "love" to walk in nature, while at the same time (unconsciously) not allowing the LOVE of the natural entities to be shown to them. As a consequence, the gap is widening between the elemental worlds of the Earth and the human family. As a result, more and more animal species become extinct and natural organisms are destroyed.

The love relationships of plants

Now, returning to my perceptual experiences in the beech grove:

What touches me first is the sensation of a lively underground activity in the grove. Inside of myself I perceive the roots of the beeches communicating by rhythmically touching each other with fine threads of light. Then, the next thing I feel is that I am being drawn into this dance of communication through a stimulation of my own grounding forces. It seems to me as if the beech trees are trying to find out how a human being who has no firm roots can ground himself.

But no sooner have I tuned into this subterranean level than the family of beeches draws my attention upwards into their crowns, as if to show me that the way the trees relate to the universal wholeness and to the spiritual levels is just as rich.

Next, I feel a horizontal force-field pulsating between the trees at my heart level. It is a horizontal field, but not a closed field, formed by individual threads that flow together from the roots and the crowns to form an interwoven unity. Again, the same phenomenon appears here too! The moment I perceive it, the interwoven current is already flowing through my body. More precisely, it flows through one of my heart centers, which I call the elemental heart (more about that later). As a human being, I am drawn into the love conversation that trees constantly cultivate and evolve with each other.

The next day, as I traveled twelve hours by train to return to the Vipava Valley in Slovenia, I was inspired to continue the communication with nature and landscapes as I had experienced it in the middle of Berlin. Standing at the window I tried to touch and caress the passing landscapes with my hands. I was surprised that the loving response reached me instantly without any delay. It turned the long and usually exhausting train journey into a pleasure. In my imagination, I stroked the shining water streams of the rivers we passed—what a paradisiacal feeling! I put my hands on the grey walls of the mountains as we passed the Alps. The mountains allowed my hands to touch the inside of their stone layers. Although all this was on a telepathic level, the communication was stronger and more loving than in the tangible world of nature. Why?

When I try to practice such exercises directly in nature, I often notice an invisible grey veil over the landscapes, thicker in some places, thinner in others. There are areas where this filter is fortunately less intrusive, but it is basically omnipresent. It is caused by people constantly projecting their reservations about nature and critically distancing themselves from this level of consciousness. This process, which has been ongoing for a very long time and has become entrenched, is reinforced by the hostile attitude of certain religions towards the elemental realms of the Earth and nature.

Actually, there is nothing wrong with the objective approach of our mind towards the world that surrounds us. In some respects, we even need this distancing in order to become aware of our attitudes towards life and in order to make decisions. But now it is time to learn when such distancing is useful and when it is disruptive to our perception of nature and to our interpersonal relationships.

Not far from the beech grove in Messel Park are two mighty solitary trees, a beech and a plane tree, surrounded by grass. The distance between the two is such that even with their mighty crowns they barely touch. As I prepared the workshop, walking between the two, I noticed a veil, invisible to the physical eye, stretched between the two trees. I suspected I had stumbled upon a river of conversation flowing between the two giant trees. It took me a long time to discover the secret of the communication between the two trees, but eventually I noticed that the beech was letting one of its roots rise up out of the earth close to the trunk and then disappear into the ground again a short distance away. This created a kind of small gate.

I lie down on the grass next to this mini-gate and imaginatively make myself as small as a thumb so that I can pass through the low gate. Behind it, I discover a small garden in the middle of which grows a miniature beech no more than 30 centimeters (11.8 inches) high—obviously the daughter of the giant beech. Focusing from the perspective of the small garden on the invisible wall between the two giant trees, I can see with my inner eye a lively traffic of communication between the two trees. I discover a myriad of tiny beings, which I perceive as love messengers, wandering back and forth between the two. They appear to me as colorful fans stretched around a light core.

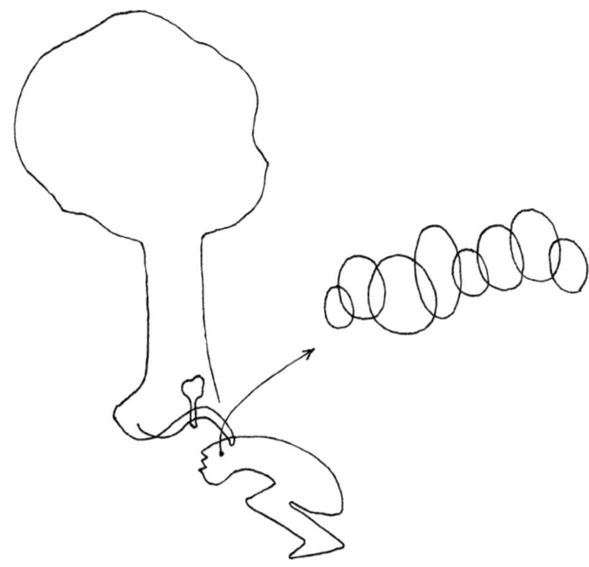

The love exchange between the giant beech and the plane tree observed from the perspective of the mini beech tree

They are so delicate that they are invisible the physical eye. But I could clearly feel that, even though the two trees cannot move towards each other like we can, they are continuously embracing each other and exchanging gifts of love with the help of these little messengers.

The Love relationships of stones, rocks, and mountains

And what about thc love relationships in the mineral world? What is their contribution to the love fields in the landscape? Before we look at the Anwa of stones, rocks, and mountains, we need to understand that they are no less alive than plants, animals, and humans, even if their outward appearance makes it seem to be otherwise. Their aliveness is, so to speak, turned inwards. Stones, rocks, and mountains are like permanently meditating monks whose aliveness is expressed through the lively movements of their consciousness.

The consciousness of stones, rocks, and mountains does not function in the way we do, by thinking and expressing ourselves. Their consciousness is one of perfect stillness and at the same time it is unlimited. The consciousness of a stone appears floating before my inner eye like a great cloud that surrounds and permeates the stone. The inability of stones to express themselves outwardly through movement is compensated for by the continuous resonating of their consciousness within the lithosphere (lithos means "stone" in Greek), a concentration of the whole potential of the mineral universe. This anchoring in the lithosphere has led the mineral intelligence to develop a great capacity to store information within itself. Ultimately, stones, rocks, and mountains in their stillness are not solitary entities but are part of the permanent flow of exchange between all expressions of the universal stone community.

I have put a lot of effort into perceiving the love fields between the individual stones and stone formations, and I thought I would find similar phenomena as they occur between the trees and plants. My search remained without satisfactory results until I understood that the stones love their mother in a similar way that small children do. We know that small children, especially when they are breastfed, are in love with their mother. In their early years, they move in delight within the mother's love field that surrounds them. Applied to the mineral world, Gaia is perhaps the beloved mother of rocks and stones.

The name Gaia (from the Greek, "Earth") is being revived today because the concept of "Earth" as it is in modern culture is closely linked to only the materialized planetary form and no longer corresponds to the image of traditional cultures that venerate the Earth as Mother, the source of all life. Thus, minerals represent the basis of creation, upon which all other forms of life later developed. Rocks in the landscape, be they small stones on the riverbanks or huge megaliths or mountains, represent the oldest generation of entities that Mother Gaia has brought forth. Therefore, the love relationships in the stone family do not take place between individual stones, but relate to the Earth's core, the pulse of their spiritual birthplace from which Mother Earth, Gaia, lets her love flow to the whole of creation.

This kind of love relationship may seem selfish at first glance, but it is not the case. It is exactly the opposite! Through their constant exchange of love with the Earth's core, stones, rocks, and mountains continuously bring the fragrance and blessing of the primal love of Gaia and her elemental entities into the landscape. This is the essential contribution of the stone family to the beauty and health of the Earth's landscapes and biotopes.

After understanding the structure and meaning of the love fields of the mineral community, the following dream bestowed on me the insight that this love dimension is also supporting trees and plants:

I am in the process of sawing tree trunks into two-meters-long (6.5-feet-long) pieces, without removing some of the small branches with green leaves. I have placed the logs side by side and raised them off the ground by placing wooden wedges underneath, with the intention of preventing rotting. With this simplistic arrangement, I expect that the leaves will continue to grow on the branches. Only at the moment of awakening do I realize that the leaves on the branches will wither, as the trees themselves no longer have any contact with the Earth.

The lesson I am taught by the dream is obvious. The permanent loving contact with the core of creation and with Gaia is just as vital for plants and trees as it is for the lithosphere of stones and rocks. I simply overlooked this dimension of their Anwa and was therefore "grabbed by the ears at night," as we say in Slovenian.

On the other hand, the dream challenged me to look more closely at whether stones, rocks, and mountains have a way of cultivating their love relationships among each other, in a similar way as trees and plants. Therefore, I went out into the landscape again to observe the Anwa of the mineral world more closely. In my perception, the love fields between stones, rocks, and mountains show a fiery quality, whereas the fields of plants are of a watery nature.

Our Vipava Valley here in Slovenia, for example, was formed on the lip of a fault. Continental movements tore apart a layer of limestone about 200 meters (656 feet) thick that covers the karstic landscape.

Thus, we live down in the valley between two cliffs. When I look up from the valley now, I see in my mind's eye how the two stone formations communicate with each other. It looks as if light waves keep forming between the two formations that have broken apart, running towards each other to "kiss" in the middle space above our valley. The two light waves jumping up and embracing each other create colorful fireworks.

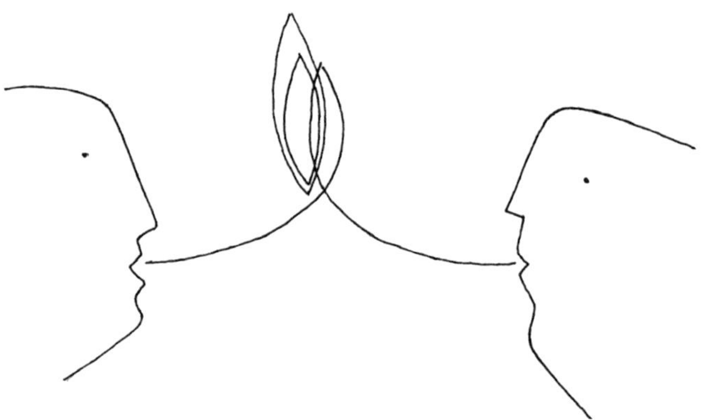

The love kiss between two stone formations

As I observe further, I notice that after this kiss, a second phase follows in which a multi-layered lemniscate in the form of a horizontal "figure eight" is enveloping the two rocky partners and enabling them to sink into a kind of silent reverie. Subsequently, the process starts all over again with the eruption of new light waves. The second phase can best be observed (using the exercises that are offered in chapter 12) with upright stones and rocks such as crystals and mountains.

4
Moon - Water - Animals

In this phase of earthly and human transformation, it is essential to depict the love fields in the landscape as extensively as possible in order to inspire people to ground themselves in a new way that resonates with the transformation process of the Earth. To ground oneself does not only mean to befriend matter as a soul being, which in itself is not easy, but to consciously connect with the love network of the Earth and its beings, and to let one's own contribution flow into the landscape and add to the multitude of love relationships. Honoring the love in the landscapes of the Earth sufficiently and granting it the place it deserves is the direct and fastest way to heal the ruined biotopes and disturbed elemental worlds.

So far, we have looked at the different elements of the love fields in the natural landscape, a richness that we usually do not even pay attention to. Yet every detail is worthy of attention. How can we look at and understand all these aspects from an overall perspective? This is where the element of water comes into play. Water occurs on Earth in the most diverse forms. Not only visibly, such as in all kinds of watercourses, lakes, seas, and the rain, but water is present more or less everywhere in the atmosphere; it enriches every kind of matter with moisture. It is in the subterranean realm as groundwater, and it moves the subtle levels of our emotional world (some speak here of "astral levels"). Its encircling sphere, the hydrosphere, we can imagine as surrounding and penetrating the whole embodied world together with all its entities. Water is thus ideally suited to connect all the aspects of Anwa and to bring its various manifestations into a continuously flowing movement.

The Earth as a hologram in water

We do not do justice to the element of water if we consider only its manifest qualities. The hydrosphere is also an elemental organism, a fine cosmic-like entity that surrounds and permeates the manifest physical Earth, including the embodied water phenomena. We could even say that the hydrosphere forms a second manifest body of the Earth. Thus, the Earth is embodied in the earth element on the one hand and in the water element on the other. Therefore, we could aptly call the hydrosphere Water-Earth.

This second Earth, the Water-Earth, is a twin Earth that is mirrored in the Moon. Why in the Moon of all places? It is the Moon that keeps the water of the hydrosphere in a constant cyclical motion with its different phases and its drawing power on the ocean tides. At high and low tide, we can recognize the visible influence of the Moon, which otherwise acts rather invisibly within the hydrosphere.

Various impressive studies and experiments have shown that water can store enormous amounts of information. Therefore, there is the possibility that all that exists on a materialized level is embodied once again in the subtle and "softer" element of water. In this context, I speak of the Earth with all its entities and life processes as a hologram in water, using the term hologram to convey that the script of life is recorded and preserved in the water sphere. The tragedy of human alienation from nature and life is reflected in the fact that our contemporary civilization bases its existence exclusively on solid and literally tangible matter, denying its own parallel existence and particular creative potentialities in the flowing water element.

As embodied beings, we are present both in solid matter and in the soft-feeling, moving hologram of water. We follow not only the binary rhythm of day and night determined by the Sun, but also the rhythm of the changing phases of the Moon with its associated movement of water. In addition, everything that presents itself as an isolated figure in the materialized world simultaneously resonates in the hydrosphere as an aspect of indivisible wholeness. Water transcends all boundaries. Water is all-connecting, all-encompassing.

In the next chapters I will speak of new organs of the heart system that cannot be physically detected, which will broaden our awareness to the fact that we are not only beings in physical matter but also exist as holograms in water. All that which cannot find expression in the

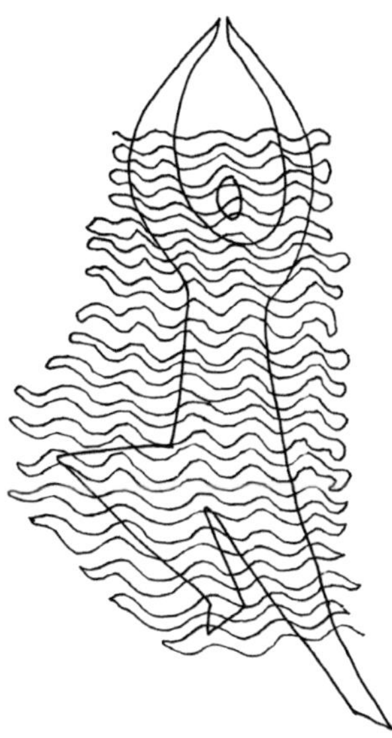

The human being as a hologram in water

material world of forms is present in the subtle body of water, not only as an idea but as a real functioning organ in the personal hydrosphere.

On the banks of the Ljubljanica River – the river that flows through Ljubljana, the capital of Slovenia – I had an inner dialogue with the elemental essence of the river and asked about the contribution of water to the fields of love in the landscape. To this end, I would like to mention that the Ljubljanica was considered sacred by the Celts, as numerous precious votive objects found in the riverbed testify. The Ljubljanica disappears and reappears seven times into the karstic rock of southern Slovenia, first as a small stream and later as a large river, and always with a different name. The disappearance of the Ljubljanica into the Postojna caves is particularly remarkable, and it is known worldwide. It becomes a living symbol of the cyclical reincarnation of life.

The river goddess answered my question by first showing herself in my imagination within the water sphere vibrating between the heights of the heavens and the depths of the Earth. She then gently and lovingly touched my horizontal system of the three hearts (which will be discussed later). The gesture was accompanied by the superimposed layered images that I translate as follows: The hydrosphere enables an ideal exchange between the love fields in the landscapes of the Earth. The causal expansion of the hydrosphere, in turn, makes it possible for the love relationships in the world to be embodied in a certain soft way. They do not remain suspended in mid-air like the concept of "platonic love" but acquire a strongly grounded, subtle body. Love thus becomes a real force that can transform the coldness of alienated interpersonal and intercultural relations and infuse them with impulses of love.

The role of animals

Observation of the various layers of the love fields in nature and landscapes has shown that all beings who find expression in the manifest world, be they stones or plants, water or human beings, embody a unique aspect of primordial love. So, what then is the contribution of animals? Since animals are found in almost all the elements and biotopes of the Earth in a variety of forms, we should assume that they also play a role in the secret love paradise of the Earth.

Unfortunately, the contribution of animals to Earth's paradise is heavily blocked. Humans have for the most part enslaved animals as livestock that fulfill their selfish desires, or the animals live as so-called wild animals in restricted habitats controlled by humans, that is, if they have not already been exterminated.

It is not necessary to describe all this in detail, as the unfortunate situation of the animal kingdom on Earth is common knowledge. It is, however, important to mention this fact because through the blocking of the animal world, a precious aspect of Anwa is lost, and its absence reveals a deep void. This loss in the overall shape of Anwa has to do with the animals' unique connections to their cosmic archetypes, partly preserved in the memory of various cultures in the form of the zodiac. But when we are walking through nature's fields of love, the primordial images of the animals projected onto the sky and their resonance with the various constellations are not our first concern. At this point we want first to know to what extent animals are still able to enrich the Anwa of the landscape under the given conditions.

Back in the 1970s, I founded an agro-artistic commune called Šempa's Family with a group of like-minded people in Slovenia. Fatima belonged to the small flock of sheep I was tending then. Now, in my imagination I passed this question on to Fatima who appeared to me now in the body of a sheep but in the upright posture of a goddess.

Fatima tells me that all the species of animals cultivate and maintain widely ramified relationships with the causal plane of the Earth. This enables the love impulses of the Mother of All Life (Gaia) to reach into the depths and heights in nature and the hidden corners in the landscapes in such a way as to continuously lift the love relationships from the causal space to the plane of the manifest world.

Fatima as a goddess

I would like to add a few comments to make my remarks about Fatima more tangible. The animals are created according to the model of certain archetypes that Gaia, as Earth Mother, recreates for each mega-epoch of her evolution to give the landscapes and their creatures a form of embodiment adapted to a given epoch. The many species of animals known today belong to our own epoch in the Earth's history. At the time of the dinosaurs, on the other hand, there were completely different animal species or body forms adapted to that epoch.

Every being that is embodied on Earth must pass through these archetypal forms and patterns on the causal plane in order to appear on the physical plane of Earth in accordance with the overall plan of Gaia's creation. This also applies to human souls who are on the path to embodiment. (This is why the signs of the zodiac can be used in astrology to gain certain insights into the character or hidden life purpose of an individual human being.)

The whole spectrum of animals from the smallest insect to the biggest elephant to the highest giraffe stands as a guarantee that the innumerable archetypes of life with all its phenomena can appear on the manifest plane in the corresponding shape. Therefore, a diversity of animal species is the prerequisite for embodied life to be present on Earth in an all-encompassing way. This also translates into all possible aspects of love relationships.

5
As a human being, am I part of nature's fields of love?

Gaia's love permeates all entities and levels of the earthly universe, so that it is hardly possible to distinguish the layers of the love fields in different entities. In principle, they are fractals of the elemental heart of Gaia, who is the Earth creator and goddess of all beings, including humans. Gaia gives specific expression to a part of her consciousness and creation so that together we form the richly structured community of the living Earth, baptized with love.

I will address the love fields of some members of this diverse community in order to broaden our access to the love relationships of the world and to gain new insights.

For Gaia's fields of love, which permeate and caress all entities and levels of the earthly universe, I originated the term "elemental heart" together with my daughter Ajra, in the 1990s. To get an idea of this, we can imagine that Gaia as mother and creator of the living Earth holds her cosmos continuously in the embrace of her love fields. The holographic fragments of this gigantic Earth heart are at the core of all nature entities and landscapes, whether manifested in a relatively solid body or invisible to human eyes.

This loving heart of the Earth appears to us as two seemingly opposing forces. One force is commonly known as gravity. The true meaning of gravity, however, is beyond the current understanding, and its significance is greatly underestimated. Gravity is the downward directed force of love that anchors the whole Earth universe within the heart center of our planet. This infinite love-force ensures that all the entities and phenomena on Earth take part in and are focused on the heart of the Earth. The other force is the creative power of the Earth's heart. It goes in the opposite direction, radiating outward in a wide fan into earthly creation, supplying all the earthly entities and phenomena with the specific love vibration of the heart. of the Earth

The elemental heart of the human being

Together with my daughter Ajra, I was able to locate the elemental heart center at the lower tip of the sternum. Furthermore, we found that the elemental heart serves as the point of origin from which the personal elemental being can move through the water hologram of the body, reaching all the limbs and organs of the body.

Elemental beings can be understood as holographic parts of the Gaia consciousness through which all aspects of the Earth cosmos are structured in order to be able to assume their life form on the manifest plane of reality. Elemental beings are the children of Gaia and are wonderful servants of life. And, although they do not possess a materialized body, in Gaia's wisdom they are nevertheless considered of equal value with animals, trees and stones. Since it is their task to reach all forms of existence from within, elemental beings can ensure their own happy, fulfilled existence (which is connected with the meaning of their essence) only in this bodiless form. In the traditional sagas and fairy tales of cultures throughout history, we encounter them as fairies, dwarves, undines, and in many other forms.

Just as animals, plants, and stones are given everything they need in their physical existence for a healthy and contented existence in the Earth cosmos, so too are all human beings, thanks to their elemental companions and servants. The personal elemental being has the task of working with our richly variegated microbiome (the community of microorganisms that exist in our body as well as the entire Earth) and translating the microbiome's energetic impulses into embodied actions.

The second function of the elemental heart is to envelop the human being with the love fields of Gaia. Parallel to the pulsation of the organic heart, the elemental love impulses are metaphorically inhaled and then distributed throughout the body. Finally, the love force-field,

The personal elemental being and the human being are one

enriched with the individual qualities, is exhaled into the environment in order to enrich the Anwa of our world.

It is important to emphasize that in the phase of inhalation not only the love impulses of Gaia as the Earth creator and her elemental entities are inhaled, but also elements of wisdom and knowledge that Gaia has stored in her field of consciousness. Therefore, the elemental heart can also be seen as the source through which insights into the laws, harmonies, and rhythms of life come to the human being (but certainly, only if one expresses an interest in them). The elemental heart, together with the elemental being, thus becomes the focal point of the personal elemental master who can help human beings to deepen their superficial path in life. We could also say that this elevates the personal elemental being to become the elemental *master* of the substantive human being. Just as it takes care of the health of our body on a personal level, the personal elemental being also knows what is and is not beneficial to the health of our larger body, the Earth.

This is a summary of my knowledge built on various experiences of the elemental worlds – see also my book *Nature Spirits and Elemental Beings – Working with the Intelligence in Nature.*

On Easter Sunday 2021, I awoke from a dream that brought me to the realization that my present knowledge of the elemental worlds should be brought into line with the current course of Earth and human transformation.

> *My family is setting off for an outing, but I decide to stay at home to give myself a few hours of rest. No sooner am I alone than a tall strong-looking young man approaches me, who was apparently already present in the house before my family left. He says he is dead tired and has to close his eyes for a minute. He throws himself forthwith on the nearest bed and immediately falls asleep. Since the room is brightly lit, I decide to turn off the light so he can rest better. As I do so, I notice that the light switch looks very worn – and also that there is a lamp still on next to the bed. Carefully, so as not to wake the young man, I also turn off this disturbing light.*

The house represents for me the living expression of the embodied human being. The dream indicates that in addition to the owner of the house someone else lives there in secret, who appears as a dead-tired young man. We can regard the house owner as a symbol for the ego or the personality of the modern human being who is constantly living, feeling and thinking in the glaring light of the mind – even when he wants to spend a few hours in silence.

I would like to make clear, however, that I have no reservations whatsoever about the ego; on the contrary, I regard personality as an aspect of human identity that is indispensable for our embodiment on Earth. Ideally, the ego should serve the human being by helping to find the way within social structures and possible upheavals. The ego is a child of the soul that grows with the experiences accumulated in the culture within which it resides.

The exhausted young man represents the personal elemental being of the human being who suffers horribly under the glare of the human mind. This suffering is not perceived until it becomes so unbearable that it affects all humanity in the form of a worldwide disease (I refer here to the so-called Covid pandemic). We are made aware that as long as we are stuck in our egocentric consciousness we will have problems recovering, despite all the proposed sophisticated pharmaceutical technologies.

The act of the dreamer in switching off the glaring light is the first necessary step to getting back into the binary rhythm that invites the personality on the one hand and the personal elemental being on the other to join in a common dance for the time span of a human life. Gradually we become aware of the need to balance the sequences of our mind-occupied consciousness with periods of inner immersion, and even better, become aware of the fields of love in nature and landscapes. The activities of the night, which are marked by the influence of the Moon and our dream narratives, should be considered to be as important as the activities of the day.

And let us not forget the other lamp, next to the bed, which is also switched off by the dreamer so that the personal elemental being can find its way back to its full form of existence. What is the significance of this act? By turning off the bed lamp, a second problem in the relationship between the human being and their elemental being is exposed. Since the bed lamp illuminates the head of the sleeping young man and will possibly disturb his sleep, we can look for a disturbance in the mental area of the contemporary human being.

To be honest, I am also subject to this disturbance. While quite a lot of knowledge about the elemental world and its subtle entities has been collected in the last decades, even about the personal elemental being, and in our groups we have also practiced together in order to perceive the elemental beings of different elements, now it is about something else. It is about us as human beings facing the challenges of the third millennium hand in hand with our elemental being. As we are crossing the threshold of the new millennium, we are caught up in a complicated vortex of world circumstances that we will find difficult to master without intimate communion with our personal elemental being.

With the concept of an "intimate communion" I want to convey here that it is necessary to dismantle the mental boundaries by means of which the human being maintains a sharp distance from their "own" elemental being for fear that a being of a foreign kind could conquer their "I". This subliminal fear prevents an honest and loving relationship from developing between the two partners who live in the same "house". However, this fear is unwarranted. An elemental being is not an "other person" but a holographic part of Gaia, a pure expression of her love and care for the human being she loves.

When I follow this thread of thought and feel inside myself—using the many facets of my (inner) elemental being, I sense Gaia's hand lovingly touching the organs of my body and caressing their archetypal forms. It feels similar to my caressing of the passing landscapes when I traveled by train to Slovenia—only this time I myself am being caressed inwardly. The elemental heart, at the bottom of the sternum, is the organ that makes this intimate exchange possible.

In order to be able to participate in the love relationships of our world, there are two portals or gates in the elemental heart of the human being. One portal is located in the back area at the level of the sacrum and enables us to breathe in the love impulses from the surrounding love force fields. The other portal is on the front of the body at the level of the solar plexus. It serves to pour out the Anwa enriched by human generosity towards the world. When these two gates are open, people can become a blessing for their environment, and at the same time they themselves are blessed by the love fields of nature and its entities.

6

The unified love field of humanity

So far, on our path to learning more about the core power of the human heart, we have moved in a realm where the human being is fully integrated into the fields of power and love of the Earth and its entities. Because of the special function of our elemental heart, we are embedded on that plane in our individual role in the manifold community of all those entities that inhabit the embodied plane of the Earth with us and are creatively active in it.

Now we have arrived at the threshold of another realm in the wholeness (holon) of the earthly heart system that is specific to the human being. This does not mean, however, that we are dealing here with a realm that is completely separated from other entities and spheres of the earthly universe. Rather, it is about the essential quality of being human, our heart aspects, which enable and support precisely what makes the human being a human being in the first place.

First, we should realize that we humans exist in two completely different planes. Our human existence develops in two different spheres of the earthly universe and oscillates back and forth between these two levels.

For a certain period of time, we live in the so-called sphere of the ancestors, who are also our descendants. We also call this sphere the spiritual world, because we exist there as souls in a subtle spiritual form of existence. This does not mean that we just float around as disembodied spirits. In my experience, people are just as active in the spiritual phase of their existence as they are during their incarnation in the physical world. In my geomantic investigations of certain places in natural and urban landscapes, I often find so-called soul paths along which souls from the beyond choose to visit certain places. They are interested in finding out what information is stored in the etheric layers of these places. Sometimes they have also taken it upon themselves to inspire embodied visitors at such places with the wisdom and knowledge that is anchored there.

In the next phase, the human soul is born into the manifest world, in order, among other things, to learn to embody and express spiritual-soul values and qualities under the conditions of matter. In this phase of material embodiment, it is particularly challenging to keep the connection with the dimension of one's own soul. The fascination of the materialized world and the abundance of tasks that we find here cause the dimension of the spiritual world to fade, so that we almost, or even completely, forget it. This development is further driven by religious and scientific dogmas that produce patterns of thought which separate the two spheres or even deny the existence of the sphere of the ancestors and descendants. In this way, the gap between the two spheres of our existence widens, ultimately leading to the loss of wholeness in the modern individual. The human being is split into two parts that essentially should belong together according to the matrix of being human.

So, let us ask ourselves if the heart, our tirelessly beating organ that symbolizes all-connecting love, could help us bridge this tragic gap between the two parts of our human nature?

A fragment of Paradise

In *Universe of the Human Body,* I made a considerable effort to expand the concept of the heart space, but apparently the time was not yet ripe a few years ago to make the leap to a truly holistic level. At that time, I could bring forth only a few aspects about the heart center as we commonly understand it, principally the dimension of the aspect located behind the back. A completely new level of the heart system was first indicated to me in a dream on March 15, 2021:

> *I am visiting my friend Austin, who died two decades ago. He served as a British diplomat at the UN in Geneva. In one of his rooms, I discover a structure made of fine grains of sand resembling three pointed tongues that is leaning against a wall. On each of their tips is a black square cube. All three cubes are positioned at*

the same height and are identical in shape, each with a round hole from which a very special light is emanating. The color of the light is golden, infused with a silvery tone, as if the sunlight and moonlight were united in it. I feel these rays of light are an expression of a quality of the heart that is unknown to me. I am so delighted that I ask Austin if I can take the right-hand cube of the three.

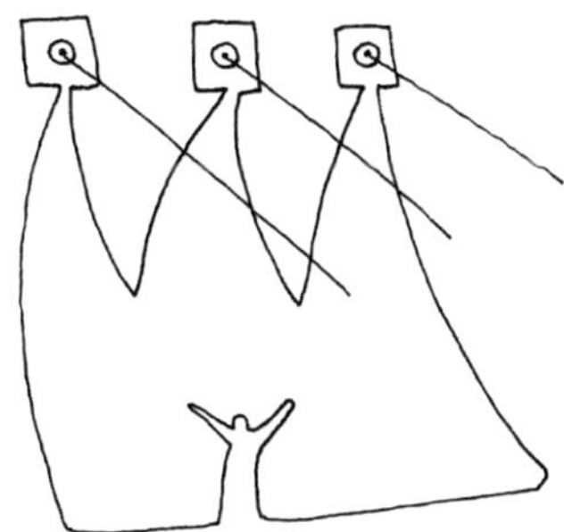

My delight at the three sources of heart power

When I thought about the dream during the following days, I could distinguish two of the three sources of heart power: the left heart muscle and the heart center in the middle of the body. But there were three cubes. Is there anything on the right side of the chest that could serve as a clue to the third cube? On the physical level there is nothing there that I could identify with a heart aspect. And yet in the dream it was precisely the cube on the right side that I wished to take with me.

It was only during my geomantic workshop in the Ruhr area in the autumn that I was able to discover the secret of the heart light source on the right. I would like to say in advance that due to the many workshops I conducted in the landscapes between Cologne, the Ruhr area, and the Sauerland, I know this area of Germany very well and was able to identify it as the heart area of Europe. Figuratively speaking, it lies on the line of the spine of the European continent, vibrating between Crete in the south and Iceland in the north. That is why it is no coincidence that I found the key to the secret of the right side of the heart center in the Ruhr area, of all places. (Actually, the Ruhr area was energetically an exceptionally radiant land before its layers of black coal were dug up. The quality of black coal is like that of a diamond!).

What I found there first appeared to me as a holographic fragment of Paradise, reminding me of the biblical story of the expulsion from Paradise. When humanity had to leave the paradisiacal dimension of our life on Earth, each individual was allowed to take a tiny fragment of the quality of Paradise. Since then, we have carried our fractal of Paradise on our right side, exactly opposite the heart muscle, serving as a signpost so that we do not lose our way on the difficult path through the patriarchal age. At the end of our path we hope to arrive safely at a new paradise, which I call "Gaia Culture" (see *Creating Gaia Culture)*.

Various religious traditions speak of Paradise as a long-gone former state of human existence, where we lived in harmony with the Earth and all the entities of nature. Perhaps this refers to the Neolithic Age of the Goddess before the influx of patriarchally organized peoples into Neolithic Europe from the third millennium BC onwards. However, anthropologists have been able to show through field research that even in our time there are still peoples on Earth who live together according to paradisiacal laws, standing by each other unreservedly and enjoying harmonious interaction with the nature entities of their companion world. Instead of fighting each other in wars, they have developed various forms of ritual confrontation. This is exactly where we want to go, by attuning ourselves to the new level of consciousness that is coming about through the present Earth and human transformation!

The fractal of the heart of humanity in me

Returning to the dream of the three cubes of heart power, I must say that I do find the paradisiacal quality on the right side of the chest to have equal significance with the other two sources of heart power. It is not only about the focus of a certain quality, but also about the point of outpouring of a very specific heart power. Is such a source of love really on the right side of our chest?

To progress in answering this question, we should take into account that we are dealing with different levels of the three sources of heart power. The one on the left is associated with the heart muscle, so it is directly related to the manifest plane. The heart center in the middle is more of an etheric phenomenon. Does the heart center on the right side perhaps "only" exist as a hologram in water? According to my findings discussed in chapter 4 on the Water-Earth sphere, all three hearts should be understood as a watery phenomenon, although the first two additionally exist either on the physical or on the etheric plane.

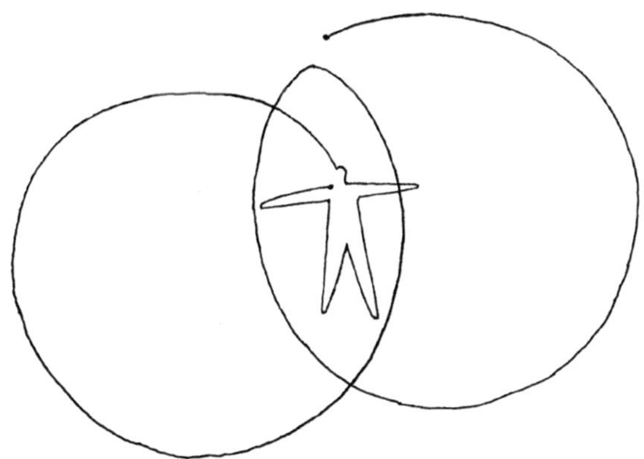

The human being is at home in two spheres of life

I would have been stuck at this point if my daughter Ana had not also written a book in the same year (2021), *Being Human in the Now,* which came about as a result of a soul attunement and telepathic dialogue with her sister Ajra, who had died ten years before. What particularly touched me while reading the book was the determination with which Ajra proclaimed that the two parts of humanity – one embodied in this world and the other alive on the other side – irrevocably belong together and form a unity. Her message is that only together, in the wholeness of our humanity, can we fulfill the meaning of our existence in the cosmos.

This led me to the realization and insight that our forgotten unity is anchored in our common mega-heart, of which every single individual of the human community – whether present on the earthly or on the spiritual-soul level – carries a part in their chest. It is this fractal of the common mega-heart of humanity that pulsates on the right side of the chest of each and every one of us.

The holographic principle implies that we are all vibrating uninterruptedly in communion with the universal heart of humanity through the mediation of the fragment of Paradise. I am sure that all the enmities associated with the mutual depredations that characterize the human community today will fall away from us when we became aware of the fact that we share in a common heart field. Love will triumph!

Unfortunately, we are still far away from this. The first thing we need to do is to dismantle the barriers I spoke about before that prevent people who are living in the body and those living in the garment of the soul from experiencing each other as a loving community. The threshold of death is used by the forces that work against the Earth and against human transformation as a means to deny the original communion of the two spheres in order the more easily to mislead those who exist on the embodied plane. I experience these barriers, maintained by prejudices of the mind and by religious dogma, as cutting through our hearts like a sword.

The external organs of perception alone are insufficient to break down these barriers. We need to develop new telepathic, imaginative and ritual forms of communication with the otherworld and to cultivate a renewed sensitivity for this purpose.

7
The organic heart is a treasure trove

If we now move from the right to the left side of our chest, we come to the threshold of the precious heart muscle. As long as our heart beats rhythmically, we can enjoy our embodiment on Earth.

In order to be able to cross the threshold and reach the background areas of the organic heart, I must return again to the images that surfaced in the dream I recounted of my friend Austin. As mentioned, there I was presented with the new composition – hitherto guarded in the causal background of the heart space – of the three heart centers arranged horizontally in the chest space of the human being. All three appeared to me on the symbolic level as black boxes with round openings from which the intensely beautiful light shone. Looking at this again, I immediately recognize that I am standing in front of a series of three love sources that I have never seen before. However, this raises three questions that have not yet been answered:

- What do the three tongues mean, on the tips of which the three sources of love are positioned?
- What does the sand that makes up the three tongues stand for?
- What do the three black boxes stand for, through the openings of which the intense love light shines?

An aspect of the dragon heart

A few months earlier, when I had traveled by train along the Rhine from Ljubljana to the Ruhr area to give a cycle of lectures and some geomantic workshops in the area between Cologne, Herne, and Berlin, as I mentioned before in connection with my telepathic relationship to the landscape, I stroked and caressed the Rhine here and there during the train journey. It happened that before my inner eye the river suddenly opened up and gave me an insight into its water body: I could see into the primordial ground of creation, where the dragons are at home.

In line with countless folk traditions, I consider dragons to be a symbol of the forces that keep the entire universal creation in dynamic motion and constant renewal. I compare it to the nuclear force, which sits silently in every smallest particle of matter and—if not industrially exploited and abusively robbed of its energy—both drives the unfolding of the universe and allows it to be decomposed again according to the cyclical principle. From my geomantic research, I experience dragons as formidable and powerful beings. Fear of their elemental power has led to them being portrayed in myths and legends as loathsome reptiles. For me, however, they resemble Titans, capable of carrying out the creation plans of their mother, Gaia, with the wisdom of a loving heart.

Through the revelation granted to me by the Rhine, it is now clear that the tripartite tongue in my dream, which sustains and nourishes the love power of the three hearts, stands for this dragon power, the primordial creative power of the Earth and the universe. And the fine sand with which the dragon's tongue is fashioned in my dream symbolizes the fact—transcending our rational logic—that dragons stand so high in the hierarchy of cosmic creation that their bodies are not only present in every atom of the universe, but they simultaneously inhabit the vastness of infinity as perfectly wholesome and conscious beings.

If the fine sand in my dream is symbolic of dragon power and also of the atomic power of the universe, where can I find in the human heart muscle the mighty heart power of the dragons, which after all should be capable of amplifying a thousand times over the power of love that flows from the human heart? Why is the love radiating from human hearts so weak that we have to watch powerlessly as wars rage mercilessly around us? The answer to these questions can be found in the three black boxes from which the intense light of love shines in my dream.

In this mind-dominated epoch of human evolution (already consigned to the past on the cosmic plane), the three boxes acted as transformers that curbed and dimmed the intensity of the primordial force rising

The female dragon – the "dragoness" of Ukraine

from the dragon's tongue in order to make it bearable for humanity in our modern civilization. The function of the three black transformers was to attenuate the primordial force, enabling mind-dominated humans to continue their semi-conscious existence without interference. The diminution of the resonance between the human heart and the dragon heart plays particularly into the hands of the powers that want to prevent people from awakening to their true power of creation and love.

But it is altogether different with the rays of love that radiate from the three boxes in my dream—there is no weakening in them! It is precisely their radiant intensity that inspired me to write this book to joyfully announce to my fellow human beings that the full love power of the human heart is about to awaken and transform the unfavorable world developments. Something essentially new has been set in motion!

According to my insight, the controlling of the dragon power ascending to the heart level is gradually being abandoned in the process of Earth and human transformation. In this I see the benevolent effect of the personal elemental being, which is attuned to the directions of

Gaia (concerning the processes of transformation on Earth). On the other hand, this process is also connected with the sources of dragon power that are located in our abdominal cavity and manifested by an estimated several thousand billion micro-organisms living and working there. This helpful involvement of the personal elemental being enables the ascending dragon power to reach the three sources of love in the heart space of the human being and to nourish them with tremendous primal force. These love sources are thereby initiated into their new role, characterized by an immensely strong power of transformation.

Returning to the theme of the heart muscle, we can say that the intelligence and life force of the dragon world vibrates in the causal background of the heart muscle. It is therefore no coincidence that the heart muscle symbolizes the deep wisdom and power of love, which is represented so familiarly by the heart symbol that we often encounter in the media world but whose real power is rarely acknowledged.

The individual matrix resounds in the heart muscle

Would it therefore be consistent to claim that our heart muscle carries in its causal background the individual matrix of each human being, since it is located on the opposite side of the chest to the fractal of the common heart of humanity? They may seem like opposites to us, but we should not forget that in matters concerning the heart and love, we are at a level where conventional rational logic fails. According to the logic of the heart, apparent opposites can coalesce in synergetic solutions.

I am assuming that the matrix of the individual human being centered in the organic heart is older than the common heart of humanity. Before we, as individual spiritual souls, decided to unite to form the community we call humanity, we were wandering on individual paths through the universe, searching for opportunities to evolve spiritually and physically. While we were on our individual paths, we heard the call and invitation of Earth/Gaia to approach and join her in her evolutionary project. Gaia's intention to express the complex qualities of spirit in matter was met with interest from many of us who were on our own individual quest around the cosmos. To join Earth, which was already far advanced in following her own plan, seemed to make sense. Gaia already had created paradisiacal landscapes of majestic mountains, shimmering lakes, rustling forests, and a plethora of animals. She wanted to further develop her creation and was looking out for beings who were relatively highly evolved in the field of consciousness in order to promote the development of a new cultural level on Earth.

It sounded like an idea with visionary overtones unique in our universe. Many of us seekers were enthusiastic about this, and so we formed a large group and negotiated a spiritual contract with Gaia. We promised Gaia to support her in the intended cultural development on Earth in harmony with her elemental and causal worlds. In return, we were given the opportunity for further individual development with the help of the elemental beings and forces on Earth. I suspect that Gaia and her elemental worlds are especially intrigued by the diversity of our individual archetypes. Our diverse human community originates from different star systems and evolutions of the universe and can therefore bring the most varied experiences and qualities to Earth. These are exactly the right conditions for cultural diversity to emerge on Earth, but this process is not easy to manage, as both the present and the past history of our civilization testify. In this process, anchored in the causal level of our heart muscle, the individual contributions of all are required.

The causal background of the organic heart appears in my imagination in a shape that resembles a snow-white drop. The heart is completely immersed in it. I would identify this "drop" with the so-called "fifth ventricle" that has been reported in some recent research. According to these reports, electrical impulses are said to continually emanate from a "fifth ventricle" that enable our heart to beat rhythmically and animate our body. If these impulses stop, life on the earthly plane is over. My understanding and insight regarding the imagination of the snow-white drop relates to the causal dimension of the fifth chamber of the heart, which I see as a space in which the spiritual-soul identity of each individual is anchored. In ancient Egypt the ID was spoken of in this context as a most important treasure house of the human being.

What worries me about the aforementioned imagination are the dark threads that bind this white drop containing the information of the human matrix firmly to the ground. If the cosmic qualities that each individual brings to Earth are to work creationally and for the good of all beings of life and light, the archetype inscribed in the heart must be freed of those bonds that endanger human freedom. To me, these ties seem to be grafted on by forces that do not want people to awaken to the full light of their hearts.

Around Easter 2021, which was dedicated to the revelation of the new heart system, I received a dream that confirmed my assumptions:

> *My wife and I are at a stranger's house, sitting down to an abundantly laid out breakfast table, which is in the shape of a mandorla (the result of two circles intersecting)—the archetypal shape that symbolizes the gate of birth. We sit on the right side of the two lateral arches of the mandorla and our host sits at the lower tip from which a piece has been sawed off (which seems strange to me). Suddenly, he grabs the two corners of the sawed-off tabletop and tilts it to the right—seemingly to show why the mother symbol has been damaged. Everything slides towards our heart spaces and blocks our heart planes. At the same time, I see that the table has a framework with four legs that are still firmly on the ground.*

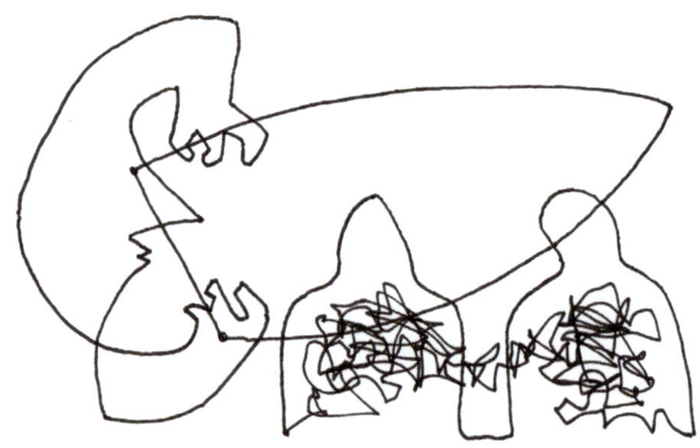

The dangerous breakfast

I connect the mandorla-shaped space with the "fifth ventricle" that I mentioned above. I am worried about the fact that although the chamber is perfectly designed, it appears lifeless. The essential quality of the heart is missing there – the richly effervescent power of love. Has the influence of the opposing force depicted in the first part of the dream penetrated so far now that the source of the love energy in the human heart is fundamentally threatened? That the problem is rooted in a deeper level is indicated by the table frame with four legs that are "still firmly on the ground."

Almost a year later – at the time I was writing these lines – I wanted to visit the fifth chamber of my dream again, to find out what is happening to the source of love in the human heart. To my dismay, I find that in my imagination I cannot enter the chamber because an oily liquid has spread around it, reaching my ankles and preventing me from opening the door. But I understand that although opposing forces can block access to our treasure of love they cannot destroy the sanctuary itself because love is a force that defies the methods of logic.

After removing this hurdle with the help of my elemental master, I can enter the mandorla-shaped chamber. This time I immediately realize that the mandorla room is the home of life. The mandorla represents both the gateway through which life is born and the seed of life. As I climb the staircase that sweeps upward to the ceiling in harmony with the shape of the room, a mirror lining the ceiling of the chamber, also in a mandorla shape, catches my attention. This time I can clearly see what is being reflected through the mirror from the depths of the Earth. Every moment, the impulse of love from the heart of Gaia is being reflected – to be more precise: life in the "fifth ventricle" is permanently created anew, giving rise to the "electrical" impulse that pours out to the four other ventricles. Life continuously flows.

I had to imaginatively enter the fifth chamber of my dream several more times to comprehend how the individual matrix of the human being is woven into this continuous birthing process. Ultimately, I was able to recognize that in the mirror, along with the love impulse of Gaia, the archetypal template of the individual human being can also be retrieved from the memory of the Earth. This confirms that the individual matrix is stored in the memory of Gaia and can never be lost, even though most people ignore the causal background of their being and waste their precious life force on trivial things. I am convinced that the matrix is lifted up into the fifth chamber at the very moment when we awaken to our true selves. Then we will be ready to move forward with the realization of our life task and fulfill the contract we have made with Gaia.

Our kinship with the heart of the animals

Without a doubt, we inherited our heart muscle in its organic form from the highly developed animals, as with many other of our bodily organs. Is this resonance with the animal heart significant for the newly awakening individual heart of the human being? Earlier in this chapter we looked at the contribution of the dragon power to the wholeness of our individual heart. But in what way does the animal kingdom add to this?

As I tune into these questions, I receive an answering image that suggests a hindrance rather than support for our heart muscle. I see myself wrapped entirely in scraps of cloth so that nothing, even of my face, can be seen. All that lives and breathes of me is hidden behind my back. What this uncanny experience shows me is that the resonance with the animal heart wants to contribute something very precious to the human heart, yet its vibration is completely subdued – the fabric completely absorbs the vibration. Something is taboo here. This unfortunate situation undoubtedly has to do with our systematic suppression of the animal kingdom, which I addressed in chapter 4 on the love fields in nature.

As I free my head from the cloth, I am faced with a new riddle. I am looking into the eyes of a ram with seven horns. Such a sublime quality of wisdom and love radiates from his eyes that I immediately recognize the presence of the Christ in them. I am deeply touched, but not surprised, because the lamb – the young ram – with seven horns and seven eyes is not unknown to me. I have dealt with this image in the third part of my book *Creating Gaia Culture,* in which I compared John's visions in his Apocalypse with today's events on the threshold

The young ram from the Apocalypse

of the Earth transformation. In this well known text of the Apocalypse, Christ is depicted in the form of a lamb that has the power to open the seven seals to the book of the future Earth and human transformation. Christ in the form of the lamb initiates what we are experiencing today.

But why does Christ appear in the form of an animal? With this question we come up against a second religious taboo. This taboo prevents us from connecting with Christ as the embodiment of love and wisdom and as a living power that now is within the Earth. Instead, we are led to believe that Christ has ascended to heaven and is living separately from us in the role of his Father's successor and as the young ruler over heaven and Earth—this is the opposite of what I felt in the presence of Christ as expressed in the ram's eyes. The ram told me that Christ did not leave the Earth, that Gaia and her elemental world integrated his presence into the body and landscapes of the Earth. The power of love and the cosmic wisdom that people called "Christ" two millennia ago has now become part of the earthly world and has significantly enriched the creation of Gaia.

Unfortunately, religious institutions developed exclusionary ideas and patterns that projected Christ back into the heavenly realms based on the so-called "ascension" concept. Yet, the name of Christ stands for all the aforementioned values and for the living, breathing consciousness behind them. The "religious twist" has deprived human beings of the support these values provide on the path of ascension when it is anchored within themselves.

The complete taboo I experienced in my dream through the "disguising" of my head applies to the human world but not to nature and its beings. The extended kingdoms of nature have become Christ's home on Earth. The cosmic qualities and powers that Christ stands for have become a part of the love power that permeates the landscapes of the Earth, the Anwa.

As we humans carry the heart we inherited from the animals on our left side, we now have the extraordinary opportunity to unite our individual wisdom and love power with the cosmic power and love of Christ and to embody these qualities in our daily lives.

8
The new heart system

My decision to devote myself to the nuclear power of the human heart was made shortly before Easter 2021, when I was given the dreams recounted at the beginning of this book. During that time, I was visiting a water sanctuary in Slovenia called Klevevž, where a lively, bubbling stream flows over a spring of hot water. Suddenly I noticed that I am standing in a circle of megaliths as old as the Earth itself. Then, I heard a clear voice: "In the near future you will be facing a global challenge that cannot be overcome without opening to the new inner expansion of your heart system that shines with the light of the stars."

It was an inspiration to urgently dedicate myself to make a quantum leap – to uncover and explore the loving strength of the heart system, of which I had only a hint. Nine days later, a dream came to my aid:

> *I am shown a simple clay vessel that looks as if it has been shaped by Mother Earth herself. I see three vertical cracks on the vessel, which immediately makes me think that it cannot hold water. Two horizontal lines are inscribed into the vessel above and below the three cracks. But as the vessel is filled with water, I am very surprised that despite the vertical cracks no water flows out of it.*

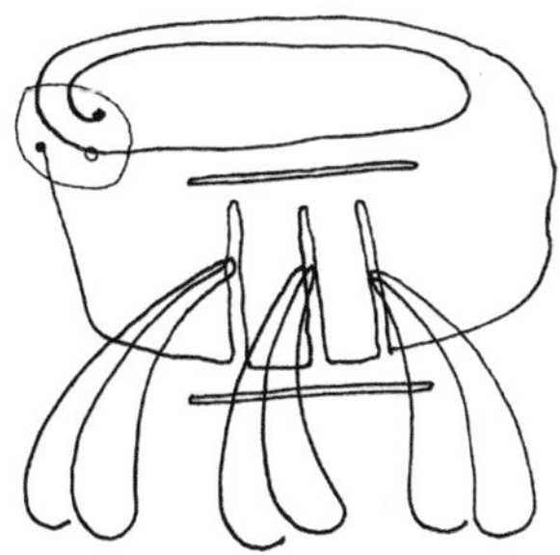

The earthen vessel with three cracks and two inscribed lines

Delving into the dream image, I realize that the three vertical cracks and the two horizontal lines were showing me the template of the newly developing heart system. Now I can relate the three vertical cracks with the three heart centers focused on a horizontal plane next to each other in the chest space. On the right side is the fractal of the common heart of the human family, on the left is the organic heart with the matrix of personal identity, and positioned in the middle is the renewed heart center—to which we will now turn. The lower horizontal line on the vessel stands for the elemental heart and the upper line for the faery heart.

In my dream I was expecting that the water of love would flow with full force out of the three cracks in the vessel. Why did this not happen?

Tuning into this question, I seek the answer with intuition. In this process, I am led from my front heart area into the dorsal space, which represents the causal level of creation. Here I observe an infinite dance of love unfolding in all directions. I see an abundance of love relationships flowing through the cosmos like a subtle yet strong network of innumerable watercourses.

Then I experience that by opening myself to the cosmic watercourses of love, I am so completely flooded by them that I am in danger of drowning. Panic seizes me. I understand that the water of love cannot (yet) flow through the three cracks because we have not found the key to balance the flow of the stream of love so that we are not seized by panic in the face of the abundance of love. A healing balancing of the renewed heart system can come about only when all its centers are recognized and operational.

In my dream, the new heart system is symbolized by the clay vessel with the three vertical cracks and the lines inscribed above and below. And so, this means that there are not only three, but five centers. So far I have described two of the three vertical cracks in more detail, as well as the lower line, which represents the elemental heart of the human being. What then is the faery heart, which is represented by the upper line?

The faery heart

When we transpose my dream template of the earthen vessel with the three cracks and two lines to the human chest cavity, we can locate the upper focal point of the new heart system at the threshold between the chest cavity and the throat. (A schematic representation of the newly forming heart system follows in the next chapter. See p. 77.). A small round depression can be found there, which I have named the "faery heart". The faery heart at the upper end of the sternum is related to the elemental heart pulsating at its lower tip. Both centers are closely related to the nature realms of Gaia. How can their different functions be described both in the heart system of the Earth and the heart system of the human being?

I received an answer to this question in a helpful dream around Easter 2021, at which time I was also gifted with most of the other dreams I have mentioned so far:

> *I am traveling abroad and wish to take a bus ride, for which I need a small amount of money in the local currency. My hostess is immediately willing to give me the money. In return, she asks me to press a certain button that is so high on the wall that she cannot reach it. Unfortunately, I am also too short to reach it. Unexpectedly, a tall woman appears who can reach the button quite easily because it is at the level of her neck.*

Clearly, the button at the level of the woman's neck points to the small depression at the top of the breastbone that I have identified as a focal point of the faery heart. The other theme addressed by the dream is the apparent lack of connection between the fare for the bus and the high button that is to be pressed. One thing is clear: the bus travels along the ground, and so, fare money, which is passed from one hand to the other, may refer to the level of the elemental heart in contrast to the button that is high up on the wall and needs to be pressed.

To press a button on a device is to set a certain process in motion. In connection with this, the task of the personal elemental being would be to supervise the transfer of forces in the body that the pressing of the button has set in motion. This implies that the role of the faery heart is in creating the causes and archetypes on the basis of which the elemental world can guide the processes of life and conceive the world of forms. Now we have left the personal level and are looking at the relationship between the faery world and the elemental world of the Earth.

As in the case of the parallel evolution of the Sidhe, the faery world should not be confused with the fairies, who are elemental beings of the air element. In English, the air elemental being is known as a "fairy" but a being working deep in the causal background of creation is called "faery". At this causal level the designation "devas" is also used for beings of the faery world who take care of the archetypes of the various plant species. The aspect of the faery world that we have in mind, however, has not only to do with plant archetypes, but more generally with the archetypes of life processes, including the love processes of the entities in landscapes and the fabric of the various cultures of the Earth. I hope this clarifies which entities of the earthly universe I am referring to when I speak of the faery world, the faery realms and the faery heart.

Now, I would like to examine some areas of activity in the faery world that I perceived with my co-worker Simona after we had attuned ourselves to each other in a telepathic way. This is particularly important to me because, while the elemental beings have gained some recognition in human consciousness in our time, the faery realms – with the exception of the plant devas – have been almost completely forgotten.

The faery realms lie deep in the background of the elemental world. If the embodied world represents the first level of living space and the elemental world the second, then the faery world would have to be sought one level below them. On this level we find the primordial beings known in Roman mythology as Parcae or Fata (goddesses of fate) and in the Greek as Moirai, who spin the thread of life. We also find them in the fairy tale of "Sleeping Beauty", where they appear as the thirteen faeries in their role as birth godmothers. They act as primal mothers of Earth's creation, weaving the archetypes of creation generated by Gaia and her dragon world into the various aspects of the living world.

The faery of the white dove of peace

We may therefore conclude that the faery world possesses the keys that have the power to shape and reshape the manifest world. This is why the faery kingdoms have been under constant pressure since the establishment of the patriarchal cultures seeking world domination. Repeated attempts have been made through magic and more recently through genetic manipulation to pull the keys out of their hands and misuse them in the interests of the ruling elites. Tragically, as a result of this increasing aggression, a wall has formed blocking off certain areas of the faery world, which are now in the shadows. In particular, two important aspects of the faery world are suffering from this stress: the primordial mothers of peace, who weave and guard the archetypes of peace under the sign of the white dove, and those – even more affected – faery beings who possess the knowledge of how the world of thoughts may be grounded. This knowledge has to do with the embodiment of consciousness in the heart. The current mind culture does not want to hear about this process because it longs for a disconnection from the Earth and its living kingdoms – a disjunction which it misinterprets as "freedom". It is in these two realms of the faery world that we are called to undertake geomantic healing work.

Another matter has to do with the role of the faery heart in the human heart system. To some extent we dealt with this at the beginning of this section when we discussed the difference between the elemental heart and the faery heart. In addition, I was shown the fundamental relationship between the faery heart and our vocal cords in our ability to produce and form speech. All the essential principles of life can be expressed and, in a sense, manifested through the word. Behind this unique ability of the human vocal organs lies the spinning and weaving of the faery world and its archetypal beings, without which no essential and meaningful words could be spoken. If, however, this process bypasses the faery heart, language runs the risk of losing its truthfulness and thus also its credibility, and it degenerates into mere gossip.

The ancient masters of the heart space

A few years ago, when I was looking at the heart center with my collaborator Simona as part of the preparations for the book *The Universe of the Human Body,* we noticed that the heart center is surrounded by microparticles. It appeared to me as if the heart center is a sun orbited by a legion of tiny planets. It further turned out that each of these "planets" embodies a certain heart quality. Some of them are bearers of those qualities of love that are significant for the manifest sphere of life, others are connected with the archetypes of the causal heart plane. They seemed to me like tiny gems, each of a distinct color and quality.

I was not aware at the time that these particles are actually entities that move and work in the relatively small heart space. However, they are not micro-elemental beings like "Gaia sparks", but some kind of minuscule "giants". I perceive them as ancient beings that have accompanied the development of the heart since time immemorial—even before the heart had begun beating in the human chest. These wise beings are obviously dedicated to facilitating the quality of the heart throughout the universe, and I will refer to them as "masters of the heart space". They have the special ability to deal with time in a flexible way, which allows them to access the time spiral at any point by opening it from within through an interdimensional portal. From here, out of this "mini-eternity", they can send their respective qualities into

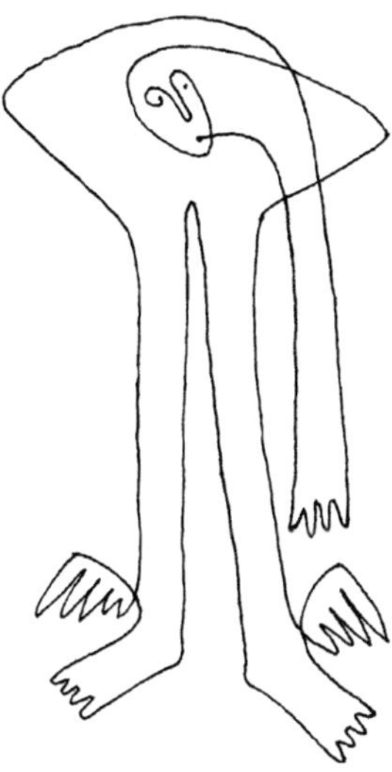

A being of the faery world grounding our thinking

the manifest life space—whereby each of the masters of the heart space embodies a certain heart quality.

After I had written about the masters of the heart in *The Universe of the Human Body,* I was given a dream which showed me that their way of working is not easy to comprehend logically. Indeed, their potent effect in imbuing the Earth's habitat with the quality of love comes from the tension between the time dimension and eternity. A love impulse that passes through the gate of eternity into the manifest time dimension is amplified millions of times, connecting there with the heart level of other beings who long for the corresponding heart quality or who are already realizing it in their lives. This creates an endless chain reaction. This is how the qualities of love contained in the five dimensions of the heart space can unfold in order to restore the original paradisiacal beauty of the Earth and the well-being of all its worlds.

So how can it be that we are still suffering from ecological stress, are surrounded by wars, and millions of human beings are threatened with starvation, when the ancient masters of the heart space, these tiny giants, possess the atomic power of love, which is as powerful in its effects as nuclear power? It is because the loving heart space has not yet been built up in human consciousness in its multidimensionality. We do not pay attention to it and do not honor it, so that the essential sphere of action of the masters of the heart has been lost. So let us strive together, as author and as readers, to grasp the multidimensionality of our heart space and to bring it to life to the fullest extent possible, reflecting the love fields of nature. Our daily exercises can help us in this endeavor.

9
The synergies of the new heart center

As we now look more closely at our model of the new human heart system, it is worth remembering that we have so far dealt with all four of the heart centers – representing the basic structure of the new heart constellation – which revealed themselves in a new way. The heart constellation has the shape of a rhombus or diamond. We began our examination with the elemental heart at the lower point of our sternum, through which we are incorporated into the earthly creation. We then turned our attention to the common heart of humanity, of which every member of the human family, whether embodied or existing as a spirit-soul, carries a fractal on their right side. The third step in our approach to the newly emerging human heart system was to look at the heart muscle and the individual love source, wherein the matrix of transpersonal identity pulsates.

Lastly, we focused on the resonance with the faery heart, which we located at the top of the sternum, at the threshold between the chest cavity and the throat. What we have not yet addressed is the middle of the heart space, usually referred to as the heart center. Given the expansion and multivalence of the heart system as described, can we still speak of a single heart center at all? According to the yoga tradition such a heart center exists – the "chakra of the heart"– which is one of the seven power centers located along the spine.

When we speak of the power of the heart or end a message with "heartfelt greetings" or declare our love to another person, we are certainly not thinking of the heart muscle, even less of the elemental heart, and certainly not of the total heart of humanity. We are thinking of a heart that does not actually exist on the material plane at all, but is an undefined bundle of heart qualities and spiritual forces summarized as a general heart symbol and visualized in the center of the chest. In the background of this mind-created heart we can sense the invisible but strong presence of the heart chakra.

Could it be that the idea of a single heart that ignores the four heart centers is an invention of the monotheistic religions emerging over the last three millennia that has swept away the motley crew of gods and goddesses from ancient times and enthroned a male-conceived god as the single ruler over Heaven and Earth? In the name of this sole deity, the power of the heart can indeed be located only in a single heart center.

The downside of this narrowed conception, which reduces the heart's power to a single source, is evident in its vulnerability to manipulation. If there is no broad-based constellation of the heart, such as revealed in the foregoing chapters, but instead the heart center is considered to be concentrated on a single point, then it is relatively easy to reverse the direction of this isolated heart center. It can thus be misused, for example, by turning the focused heart force in a dark and destructive direction in order to create conflicts and wage heartless wars against nature or against our fellow human beings.

The duality of good and evil, which is the characteristic feature of the old heart, can be overcome only by the complete renewal of our heart system in which the different and autonomous heart centers work together synergistically. As shown in the diagram on the following page, each of the four heart centers pulsates on a different level of the multidimensional body space and beats in its own rhythm. When these four rhythms are brought together, the new heart center emerges, capable of shining with the power and wisdom of a thousand suns and moons. Now, what is the driving force or consciousness that can achieve this synergy, through which the new heart center will be born? At this point the idea of the "third eye" comes into play.

The role of the third eye

Many cultures recognize the term "third eye", which is often indicated as a round mark centered between the eyebrows. In my experience, the third eye is not a single center of consciousness, but a series of three power centers in our cranial space. I perceive the third eye as a horizontal channel of power and consciousness that connects the back of the head with the forehead.

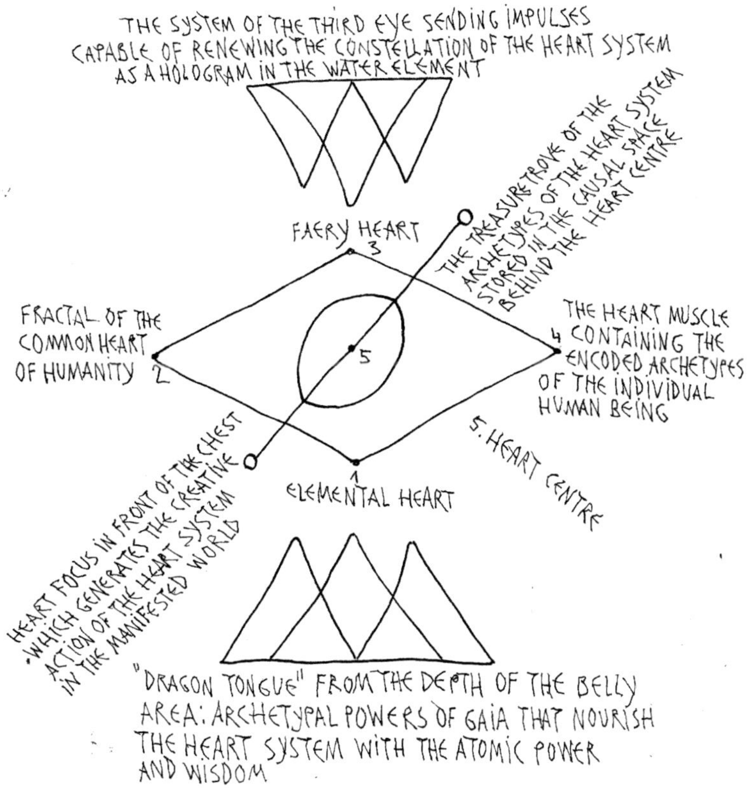

Schematic representation of the newly developing heart system

At the back of the head is a focal point of connection with the world of ancestors and descendants. Opposite this point, on the forehead, is a focal point between the eyebrows that orients us in the causal background of the physical world. In the middle of the cranial space is the center of consciousness, the place where Gaia knowledge communicates with the wisdom of her cosmic counterpart, Sophia – the wisdom from the primordial beginning. This is the actual center of the third eye.

This tripartite third-eye system is the source of consciousness by means of which the entire structure of the new heart system is maintained in the memory of the body and its elemental being.

Were the third eye system to fail to sustain the new heart constellation as a geometric matrix and fail to remind our individual elemental being of its role in the overall composition, then the individual "stars" of the heart constellation would be at risk of detaching and moving away from each other to continue along their own developmental paths. The new heart system as a symbol of hope for a happy and peaceful future would disintegrate, since it can only continue to exist through the precisely attuned synergy of all the centers, qualities and forces involved.

However, this synergetic interaction in the new heart system is not yet sufficient on its own to constitute the new heart center. Consciousness belongs to the air element and therefore does not have on its own the dynamism required to imbue the synergetic processes of the new heart system with enough driving force to enable the expected elemental power of the new heart system to unfold. The contribution of the dragon powers is required for this, and these powers are attuned to the impulses of the third eye.

Consequently, the new heart system, and thus also the new heart center, develop with the help of two simultaneous synergetic processes, the working together of different forces. The dance of the four new heart centers takes place on the causal plane pulsating behind embodied reality. However, the interplay of the third eye system, which is bundled up in the cranial space, and the dragon force, which operates out of the abdominal cavity, takes place in the deeper dimension of the causal world that I call the "primordial space of eternity". The embodiment of the heart forces and their qualities, which flow from our heart center once the two synergetic processes have set the new heart in motion, can develop only in the context of the individual human being, and ultimately of humanity as a whole. But are we ready to become complex sources of love in everyday life ourselves?

The elemental angels

Does the role of our third eye have an equivalent in the landscape? This question is essential and must not be avoided because we want to get to know not only the new heart system in humans but also how it manifests in the love sphere of the landscape. During my workshop at the Hibernia Waldorf School in Herne, Germany in April 2022, we visited the Katzenstein, a place above the Ruhr, south of Bochum.

Here is a forest that is unusually rich in holly (ilex) trees, which can easily recognized by their shiny, thorny evergreen leaves. For me, it is the plant with the strongest relationship to the cosmic vastness of the universe. To connect with the inner being of the holly plant, we reproduced the characteristic shape of the holly leaf—its so-called signature—with our hand, stretching and clenching our fingers to "engrave" the characteristic holly leaf several times into the ether with our "pen". Afterwards, we enjoyed the dancing presence of the elemental beings accompanying the holly in the midst of our circle. As we felt into the silence, I perceived a group of beings in front of us. They were invisible to the physical eye, of course, but because of my deep experience with such phenomena, I recognized them as elemental angels. We stood silently facing each other—our group as embodied human beings and their group as beings of another dimension—both of us with uncertain futures, reflecting within ourselves the long-lost knowledge of our fellowship.

When I refer to these elemental beings as angels, I am not referring to entities from the religious traditions. For me, angels are creative focal points and entities of the universe that correspond to the elemental beings of the Earth. They ensure that the universe can continually develop and change according to its cycles and rhythms. Since the Earth is a holographic fragment of the universe, angels are also active on Earth in various ways. Some of these entities even took on the subtle body of elementals created and offered to them by Gaia—in the same way that we humans took the opportunity to evolve in the animal body by using it as our temporary home. Embodied in the etheric body of these elementals, the elemental angels were able to move much closer to the manifest world than the angels who do not inhabit an elemental body.

The Judeo-Christian tradition regards these elemental angels as "fallen" angels and calls them "cursed by God" because they have supposedly come too close to the Earth. Behind this idea lies the mindset of a bygone era that understands matter and spirit as opposites, that subordinates matter to spirit, and consequently regards the Earth as unworthy to be home to angels and other entities of the spiritual world. It is one of the tasks of geomantic healing work to free the elemental angels from the weight of this curse so that they can resume their precious activity on Earth unhindered.

Today, the elemental angels can be appreciated as landscape angels who maintain the sacred identity of individual landscapes of the Earth and supply them with energy from the high cosmic sources. This includes the source of universal love power, which is embodied in the Judeo-Christian tradition by the seraphim. Thus, the elemental angels offer their precious contribution to the all-encompassing quality of the fields of love in the landscape, in nature, and among human beings, enriching them with the cosmic quality of seraphic love.

Another gift that the elemental angels bestow on human beings in this perilous phase of Earth transformation is their willingness to serve as elemental guardian angels. Guardian angels are acknowledged in the Christian traditions, but in this case, they appear in an elemental form that enables them to move closer to the danger zones of the dissolving material world, making their protective activity more effective. (See the exercise that I suggest for summoning their protection, p. 115. It should not be overlooked!)

The heart center as an interdimensional portal

The model of the new heart system and its embodiment that has been revealed in this book so far may be descriptive and logical, yet it does not satisfy me completely because it does not yet explain how the new heart system might affect our companion world. The chaotic situation of our world torn apart by opposing forces was, after all, the reason to set out in search of a new heart system. Have we somehow ended up in the wrong place?

I do not think so. However there is another essential component and extension of the heart that we still need to investigate. This is the horizontal connection of the heart center through which the space behind our back is connected to the space in front of our chest. The dorsal space represents the causal dimensions of the embodied world—where the primordial patterns of life reside that create the manifest (embodied) world environment.

For the new heart system to be effective in the world, it should be recognized as an interdimensional portal that helps to transform certain important aspects of the world order and world events. Since we are dealing with the heart here, this certainly involves those qualities that we addressed in connection with the individualized "stars" of the heart system, which are capable of building and transforming the physical realm into a world of paradisiacal quality characterized by loving relationships.

I would like to point out here that the term "interdimensional portal" does not refer to a simple passage between the different dimensions of a multidimensional reality. In architecture, the entrance area of a building is called a portal when it possesses certain characteristics. We can imagine the portals of certain medieval churches, especially cathedrals, for example, with dogtooth designs resembling an accordion. The series of arches may house columns or figures of saints in the interstitial spaces. A Gothic portal built according to this accordion principle forms contracted vestibules through which the faithful pass in order to attune themselves to the different dimensions of the sacred space they are about to enter.

The term "interdimensional" in the context of a portal refers to precisely these kinds of antechambers that an impulse issuing from the causal world has to pass through in order to emerge and become active as a creative impulse or action in the embodied world. In our own case, we are dealing with four such antechambers that enable the heart center and the individual it belongs to, to act as an agent of love in the world. These are the individual aspects of our heart system that we have now learned about. They are arranged in pairs like the portal of a cathedral with its niche arches and symbolic figures arranged to the right and left:

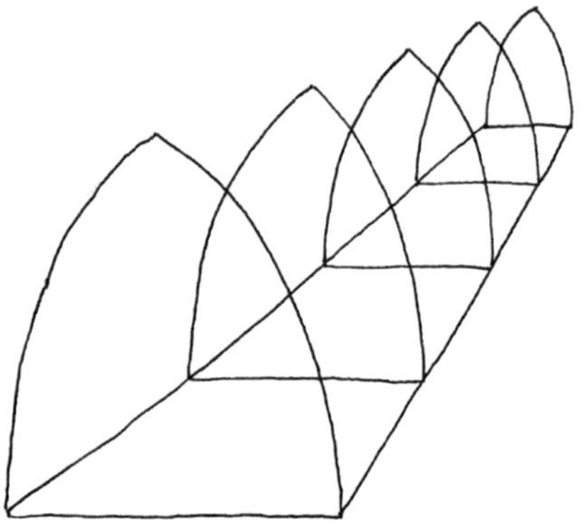

A Gothic portal built according to the accordion principle

- The first pair refers, on the one hand, to the elemental forces of the Earth (the dragon's tongue), and on the other hand, to the cosmic consciousness, focused in the system of the third eye.
- The second pair consists of the individual soul matrix (the heart muscle) and the fractal of the universal heart of humanity.
- The third pair are the faery heart at the upper end of the sternum and the elemental heart at the lower end.
- The fourth pair refers to the two spaces of the heart center that we mentioned above. These are the focal point in the dorsal space, which stimulates the relationship with the causal world, and the focal point in front of the body, which anchors the described portal system on the manifest world plane.

A portal is not only used to enter a building, but also to leave it. In the case of the heart center, this twofold function of a portal can be graphically represented as follows: When a human being perceives the need for a love impulse in our companion world, the resulting call passes through the four antechambers of the heart space to be perceived by the eight heart qualities mentioned above. The network of heart qualities is now scanned for the corresponding love force that would be able to answer the call. Once it has been found, the love impulse must again pass through the four antechambers of the heart portal on its way back in order to reach the manifest world.

From now on we will speak of the portal antechambers in relation to the four portals of the human heart space. In geomancy, the term portal is used to describe the gateways that enable communication between the different extensions of the Earth and the universe. In our case we are dealing with four such portals, which together enable the heart system to communicate with the manifest world.

However, the return path through the four heart portals is configured differently from the entrance to the heart system that I just described. The heart properties and powers should be incarnated now, be it in the sense of a loving relationship or a healing or creative deed. The deed of love stands to become a concrete action and even to take on a tangible form. On the way back through the four heart portals, the deed of love is set to become so potent in its impact that it can "move mountains", as Jesus of Nazareth reportedly said.

Which entities or forces are able to imbue the four heart portals with the power that Jesus of Nazareth described? According to the traditional knowledge of many cultures, it is the mission of the four elements – water, earth, fire, air – and their elemental beings to be the agents for the process of embodiment, be it the manifestation of subtle embodied forms or materialized bodily forms. The particular balance among the four elements decides what form the particular manifestation will take. Equally decisive is the relationship of the four elements to the "fifth element", which in our case can be likened to the above-mentioned eight qualities of the new heart system and their synthesis in the center of the heart.

The four elements find their expression in the human body in the form of a constellation of energy centers (chakras) that are arranged in four circles and encompass the whole body. Each of the four circles resonates with one of the four elements. The first circle is associated with the element of water, the next with fire. To experience the centers of the earth element in the form of a circle, we need to stand up and stretch out our hands and feet. Our chakras pulsate on the inside of the elbows and on the inside of the knees. The outermost circle is in resonance with the air element, and the chakras are situated in the center of the soles of our feet and in the center of our palms. More detailed information on this subject can be found in the third appendix of my book *Dancing with the Earth Changes*.

The four circles of the elemental chakras are arranged around the heart center, which represents the etheric principle as the fifth element. Now we know that the heart center connects and focuses all the other qualities of the heart system. This clarifies the relationship between the four elements as masters of embodiment and the complete heart system of the human being, and it integrates the activity of the four elements into the new heart system. The whole human being from the soles of the feet to the center of the air element pulsating above the skull is one living heart system.

Now that we are aware of this wonderful fact are we mature enough to take responsibility for the power of love as the original quality of life on Earth?

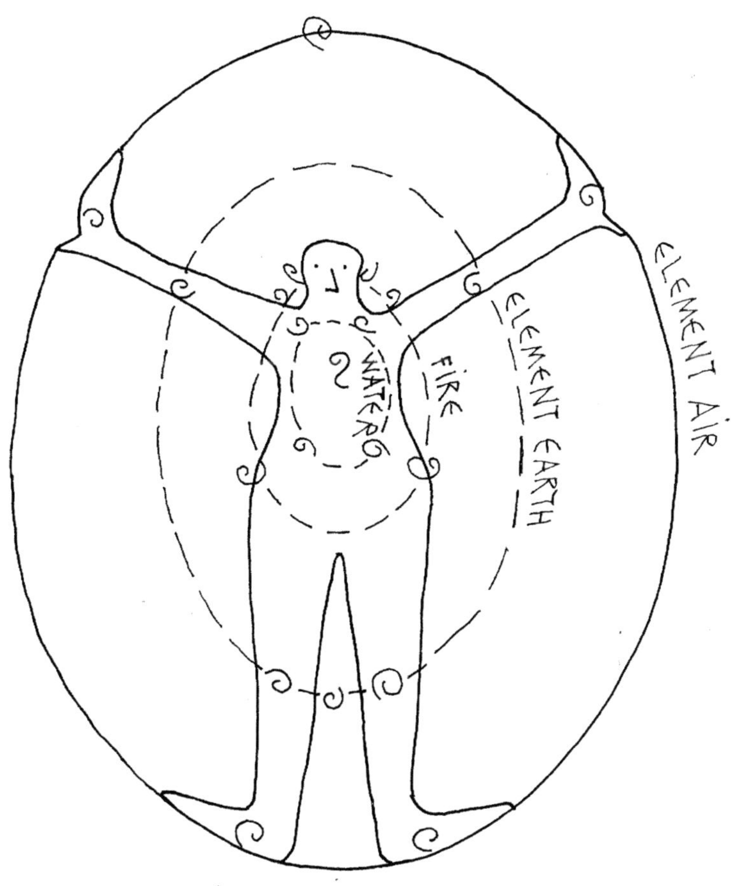

The chakra system of the four elements

10
The philo-sphere – The sphere of love

Although from the last chapters it may seem that love is mainly a phenomenon to do with human beings, this is by no means the case. The beginning of this book showed that love is first and foremost a phenomenon closely connected with the Earth creator, Gaia, with her beings and the earthly sources of love. My inspiration tells me that love represents one of the many spheres from which not only the causal but also the manifest space of the Earth is composed.

When we look at the individual spheres of the embodied Earth, it makes sense to begin with the lithosphere, the sphere of stone that constitutes the materialized Earth body and supports the whole manifest world. Next, is the atmosphere, which provides us with the air that we breathe. Then, the hydrosphere, the all-pervading watery sphere, which enables the manifestation of life and thus the development of the biosphere, which permeates and sustains all living things on Earth. The structuring of the manifest world also includes the noosphere (Greek "noos", consciousness), which is synonymous with Gaia consciousness. Gaia permeates all entities and dimensions of her manifest and causal world with her consciousness. The noosphere endows all the entities belonging to the world-cluster of Earth with different qualities of consciousness.

Here I would like to introduce another sphere, which clearly also belongs to our embodied Earth planet: the philo-sphere or the sphere of love. The Greek verb "philein" means "to love", from which the word "philosophy" is derived, "to *love* wisdom (Sophia)".

The following descriptions and exercises will be an introduction to the phenomenon of love as a distinct and holistic sphere in which not only human beings but also other entities and extensions of the earthly world-cluster participate on their respective levels and dimensions. We all bathe in the love that originates in the heart of Gaia's creation and extends everywhere. But we can also consider all entities of both the manifest and the causal dimensions of the Earth as independent potential sources of love. These love sources complement each other and nourish and enrich the philo-sphere.

In this book, I give more attention to the heart system in human beings—as our personal source of love—because whether we destroy the Earth or help to shape it depends largely on the timely awakening of the love potential of humanity. In the present epochal process of Earth change in which we are partaking, we play a crucial and decisive role that will ultimately determine the fate of the entire earthly world-cluster.

In line with this vision of the philo-sphere as developed and illuminated from various aspects in this book, we may recognize that all beings of the earthly world-constellation are permeated and entwined with a strong, as well as sweet, quality and power of love. This seems to apply to all life, with one exception. When we view the human world from the outside, instead of love and happiness we see humanity often permeated with destructive and terrifying forces. Love relationships among human beings are constantly examined and written about, but in reality, have human beings divorced themselves from the philo-sphere of the Earth?

The female-male love relationship

Starting in the third chapter, we began to move through the causal world of the philo-sphere, where the potential of the quality of love is realized by certain entities such as trees and elemental beings on the earthly plane of existence. Human beings are usually bathed in the philo-sphere through short or long-term love relationships. While wandering through the love sphere of Gaia and her entities, I asked myself which preconditions would have to be met for humanity to participate consistently and wholeheartedly in the philo-sphere of the Earth universe and thus in its auspicious wholeness.

The following dream that took place in February 2022, a time when I was working intensively on this book, led me to look more closely at female-male relationships in this particular context.

A woman and a man are lying on a table that resembles a massage table which is suspended high above a deep precipice and is held in place by two ropes that are attached exactly in the middle of each end of the table. The balance is so precise that the table would tip over if even a small amount of weight were placed on the left or right side.

In the dream I suddenly realize that I am the man lying on this balanced table together with the woman. And then, at first with a sense of wonder and then increasing to an existential dread, I feel that the table is not hanging in perfect balance after all, but is tilting more and more to one side, to the male (yang) side. I feel that I am sliding into the abyss. I ask the woman lying next to me to hold me, but we are both starting to slide into the abyss together.

At that moment, the woman decides to stand up. She now stands upright and strong on her side of the table. To my surprise, the table regains its balance. Even though one would expect the table to tip to the female (yin) side—this does not happen.

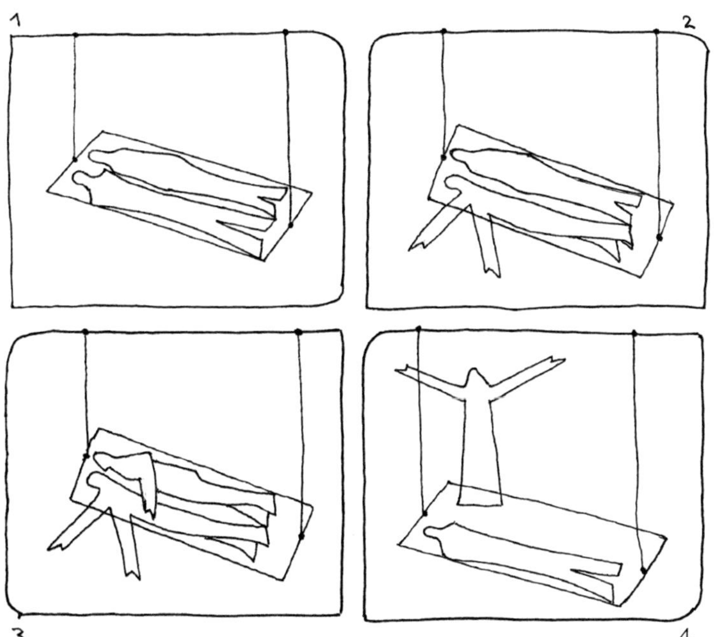

A woman and a man balancing on a table

In retrospect, I experience the woman's rising up as a resurrection of the goddess. After being saved from falling into the abyss and I am lying safely on the balanced table, I understand that I was representing the masculine aspect of the human being and that the goddess standing up next to me was showing me how to renew and activate the disintegrating sphere of interpersonal relationships.

To decode the dream from the beginning: The first sequence of the dream visualizes the female-male balance (yin-yang balance) as the foundation for maintaining female-male love relationships. It is showing how subtle and vulnerable the relationship between the two poles is. In mythical traditions the perfect balance between woman and man was during the time in Paradise, as the original time when there was still a perfect balance between all the participants in the earthly world-cluster. Paradise, however, is not just a bygone era, but the fundamental quality of existence that is uninterruptedly present in the deepest causal background of all that exists.

I become aware of being part of this balance in the second sequence of the dream, which confirms the presence of the paradisiacal quality manifested in the perfect and sustained balance between the feminine and masculine poles. But while this paradisiacal quality of balance permeated everything in the mythic time of Paradise, it has now retreated deep into the primordial ground of being. The dream sequence transfers qualities from the realm of eternity into the present and thus challenges us to restore the disturbed balance on the manifest level.

The dream is silent about what has happened between images (2) and (3), when I was overcome by the feeling of sliding inexorably into the abyss of nothingness. So, what caused the loss of security in the womb of cosmic balance, when the fear of falling into the unknown penetrated me? Since the dream offers no insight into this mystery, I shall refer to the biblical account of the expulsion from Paradise. This tradition can help our search for the background of that tragic loss—whereby paradise is to be understood as a perfectly balanced space in which all aspects and entities of the Earth cosmos vibrate in harmony with each other.

According to the Bible, God stipulated that the inhabitants of Paradise may eat everything except the fruit of the tree of knowledge. If they were to eat the apples from this tree, they would become self-confident beings, and thereby they would endanger God's supposed hegemony over the universe. The woman, Eve, was brave and self-confident enough to pluck the apple from the forbidden tree and to eat it. She handed the apple to the man, Adam, and encouraged him to bite into it as well. It was this twofold symbolic gesture of the woman that ushered in a completely new phase of evolution for the human race, enabling us to gradually grow into autonomous creative beings in the course of time.

But as human beings became self-aware and were able to act independently, the dark side of the human being emerged. Instead of maintaining and protecting the balance between the male and female poles that was won in Paradise, the male side wanted – although it seems completely unrealistic – to appropriate the woman's ability to give birth to life. This has led to the female's creative abilities being stolen and misused to build autocratic kingdoms and false democracies. Women were shamelessly degraded in interpersonal relationships and in society so that men could use the yin powers indefinitely. This is, in essence, the story of the "expulsion from Paradise".

As a society we are now standing where the warning in my dream begins. The disturbed balance between man and woman could plunge us all – and not just us humans – into the abyss. This is not only about the disturbance of the female-male balance, but consequentially also about a disturbance of the cosmic yin-yang balance. The supposed equality of women in modern societies that is politically promoted today is superficially conceived and only partially sustained. My dream tries to point out a more profound solution to the riddle of the disturbed balance. The message of the dream proclaims the resurrection of the woman as the daughter of the goddess. When she rose to her full stature in my dream, the world found its balance again.

Let us continue to explore the question of what history can contribute to the female-male balance with our theme of female-male love relationships and the discovery of the philo-sphere in interpersonal relationships.

With the final image (4), the dream reveals that the love sphere of the embodied human being, whether woman or man, is based on the female-male polarity of the yin-yang principle, according to which female-male relationships are not linear but reside in the different fundamental qualities of the two poles within each of us. As I lay rescued on the table as the representative of the masculine pole, the woman rose and stood beside me as an embodiment of the qualities and forces that testify to the continuing possibility of renewing the philo-sphere of interpersonal relationships.

This suggests that Eve, in taking the step of transgressing the taboo of picking the fruits of human freedom, also sets her partner, Adam, on the uncertain path of free will. What, then, can the female pole in human beings accomplish in these times of perilous "climatic changes" that threaten to plunge us, along with our love relationships, into the abyss of being?

I would like to emphasize here that in the causal background of a man, the feminine aspect is almost as strong as the masculine, and in the same way, on this level, the masculine aspect of a woman can be almost as strong as her feminine nature. This is why it can easily happen that a man falls in love with the female aspect of another man, or that a woman falls in love with the male aspect of another woman. It is from the point of view of the philo-sphere that female-female and male-male relationships cannot be excluded.

At our present stage of development, a decisive step of the kind that Eve took in Paradise would require that the feminine aspect within both women and men is recognized as belonging to the daughter of the goddess – in our case, a daughter of Gaia. This means:

- We must break the taboo – referred to above in the story of the "expulsion from Paradise" – by firmly rejecting the claim that the man (including the male part within the woman) is the primary creator and his female partner is only a passive supporter of his activities and glory.
- Women are free to discover in their inner world the creative forces and inspirations that reflect the new aspect of Gaia, here called Blue Gaia, which honors Gaia as a creator in the process of transforming the earthly universe. I write about this in detail in my book *Creating Gaia Culture*.

Gaia as the creator – Blue Gaia

- For this, it is necessary to recognize and realize the multi-dimensional heart system within oneself, to which this book is dedicated. In doing so, I have the aspect of Gaia as goddess of love, Green Gaia, in mind, which connects the countless spheres of love of the different worlds and beings into a unified philo-sphere of the Earth.

Gaia as the goddess of love – Green Gaia

Should the man—even the man inside the woman—now simply lie passively on his half of the table and wait until the awakened woman lifts him into the embrace of his heart space? Not at all:

- Men – and the masculine aspect in women – need to learn to become beings of truth again and to speak out, even when it comes to everyday issues, so that we live and act in harmony with cosmic wholeness.
- The man – and the man in the causal sphere of the woman – needs to become the guardian of loving interpersonal relationships, including relationships between different ethnicities and nations.

The structure of the philo-sphere

In the light of the divine extensions of the philo-sphere presented here, it is clear that the Earth's sphere of love possesses a sacral quality that we have not yet addressed, which is not "merely" one of the spherical bodies of the Earth (lithosphere, atmosphere, hydrosphere, biosphere, noosphere). It contains a mystery that must not be overlooked.

According to insights that were unexpectedly revealed to me during the writing of this book, the Earth's sphere of love has come about through its collision with a star, which I experienced as a cosmic love affair. Earth met a partner and integrated that partner into its planetary body. This happened in an epoch when Earth did not yet have a solid body as it does today, nor did it have a watery body as it did in the epoch of Atlantis. It must therefore have happened during the much older epoch of Lemuria, when Earth existed as a light body. During this cosmic collision – a sacred marriage between the feminine and masculine primal principles – an explosion of light conceived countless "children" in the form of spheres of sound and light. It is possible to sense these as the deep origin of the sacredness of many power sites on Earth. I suspect that the early peoples on the Earth discovered these places over time and recognized them as sacred places. Dancing, music, and rituals were celebrated there. Subsequent cultures have placed new layers of sacredness over them, often without knowing where the sacred quality of such a place came from.

One of the characteristics of sacred places of this kind is the special quality of light. It is as if the light of the Moon and the Sun – as we experience them today – were united. The second special feature of these "children of love" is their sound character. Their light is not only present as light, but also has an inaudible sound. They resound continuously, each differently, and together they create a harmony of the spheres that is fundamental to the existence of the Earth's philo-sphere.

The specific sound character of places grounded in cosmic love can be experienced in a Gaia Touch exercise, which I give here a new name in this context as my understanding broadens. This exercise is a gift from the landscape deva of Siena, Italy:

Gaia Touch exercise

to perceive a place by its inaudible sound

- With your hands in front of you and positioned on each side of your body, clench your fingers to a point at their tips.
- Now bring your hands towards each other, opening the fingers
- When your fingertips meet, they are open as wide as possible.
- The moment your fingertips touch, imagine two cymbals colliding.

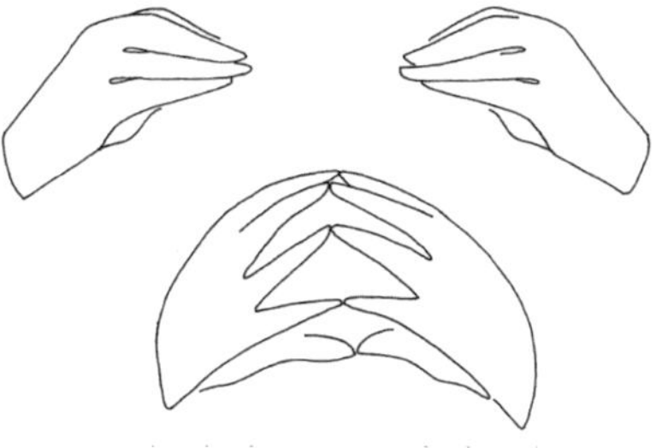

- The inaudible sound that emerges this way creates resonance with the philo-sphere of the place.
- Repeat the exercise a few times, then listen within to perceive the expanses of the place in relation to the philo-sphere.

Another special feature of the places that act as focal points of the philo-sphere on the Earth's body is their geometric character, which can be referred to as "sacred geometry". Again, we are not dealing with tangible phenomena but with a subtle balancing of various expressions of the local philo-sphere, which are generated by geometric forms and proportions. With the help of the systems of equilibrium that build up at every moment, the sound patterns of the philo-sphere are ordered and made available for embodiment in love relationships – in nature, among the entities of the Earth universe, and within the world spheres that exist parallel to each other.

I have always tried to identify and to describe as much as possible the beings that guard and nurture the various aspects of the Earth universe. Are there also entities of the philo-sphere in that sense? Yes, but they are barely perceptible – almost transparent. Their characteristic is that they are "one-eyed", this being equivalent to the "third eye" in humans. In this case, the beings of the philo-sphere see with this "third eye", just as we do with our two eyes. What I can perceive of their presence is a slightly curved upright line, perhaps their spine, which shows an anchor point at the bottom and an eye at the top. The anchor point serves to keep the Earth's sphere of love rooted in its mineral (litho) sphere, so that its subtle nature does not cause it to leave the Earth and get lost in the vastness of the universe. Around the eye are seed-like focal points from which impulses emanate continuously to stimulate the blossoming of the philo-sphere at various levels.

Are there love-sphere entities within our newly emerging heart system as well? Yes, there are! These are the tiny giants to whom we have devoted a section in the context of the new heart center; they are the ancient masters of the heart.

Entities of the philo-sphere

The heart centers of Gaia

How does Gaia maintain and nourish the Earth's sphere of love in the manifest world today? In the holistic ecology of modern geomancy, we understand the concept of a heart center in relation to a place. We usually locate the heart centers in a landscape through resonance with the human heart center. Are there hitherto unmanifested focal points of the heart that are immanent in the landscape, that become perceptible in tandem with the revelation of the new multidimensional heart system in the human being?

While I was writing this book, I received a partial answer during a workshop in Vienna dedicated to the new heart system in the urban landscape. As I was preparing the workshop, together with my co-workers Gudrun and Maja, I discovered several such heart sources in the parklands of Vienna. Apparently, the intention of their being activated by Gaia in this dramatic period of world transformation is to renew the philo-sphere of the city. Thanks to these new sources of love, I was able to assign a certain quality to three of them, although much more research is needed to explore the philo-sphere of the urban landscape.

In the public garden (Volksgarten) near the imperial palaces, we found three heart springs arranged in a row, reminiscent of the three-heart system in humans. Clearly, this is not a projection of the new human heart system onto the landscape. But the composition of the three heart centers is precisely adapted to what Gaia wants to pour out as her gift of love to the urban landscape and its inhabitants in the present epoch.

The three Gaia hearts are connected by a unified love field that I sensed at the level of my own elemental heart. This love field – "Anwa"– resembles a multi-layered field of plasma that feels like a synthesis of the elements water and air.

In the garden is a white marble building, a modern copy of an ancient temple, that represents the middle heart center. Through inner images and intuitions, we understood Gaia's intention to create a subtle spherical space in this place, where human beings embodied on Earth and those in the spiritual world could reconnect (see chapter 5). Gaia creates a white sphere of love in such places to enable the Earth-embodied and the soul beings in the spiritual world to experience each other once again as a unified human family endowed with a common heart.

The second heart center, to the left of the temple, is a huge plane tree that has a spherical protuberance on its trunk inscribed with a sign in an unknown language. By means of this plane tree, Gaia maintains a vertical-frequency ladder to enrich the love field with its different dimensions between Earth and sky. I believe these kinds of heart centers exist to ensure that the emerging love fields inspire all entities of life, including humans, to carry the quality of the philo-sphere into the expanses of the earthly universe. This gives the Earth's love force a world-creating component—a gift from Blue Gaia.

The third heart center in this series appears geographically in the form of a three-part garden complex dedicated to the Austrian empress known as Sissi. In the causal realm behind the garden complex, we discerned Gaia's intention to lovingly lead humanity to the discovery of its true self through the possibility of embodiment on Earth. The first part of the layout of the garden—a star with a sphere in the middle—awakens in the soul the desire to descend from the etheric plane to the embodied Earth. The second sequence of the garden lies in a depression of the landscape and stands for immersion in the world of matter. The third space, in the shape of a rounded apse, is where the human being is infused with the love of Green Gaia and together with his trans-illuminated body is lifted to the level of his true self.

I will give an example here of a sacred place that shows traces of the cosmic collision mentioned above, interpreting it as a sacred marriage between the feminine and masculine primordial principles, and ultimately as the origin of the Earth's sphere of love. Lake Bled, which is one of the most popular tourist places in my native Slovenia, is known for the island in its center dedicated to the Holy Mother Mary. In the not-too-distant past, this island was one of the most important places of pilgrimage in my country. Traditionally—that is, before its Christianization—the sanctuary of the Slavic goddess of love was located there.

During my geomantic workshop in Bled in June 2022, our group tried to perceive how this place reveals traces of the sacred wedding.

In order to be able to perceive the deep layers of the island—which is actually a huge rock in the middle of the lake—we telepathically lifted the rock a little bit.

At that moment, I find myself pulled into the depths below the island by a whirlpool of water. There I see a tall ruby-like crystal. I sense that this crystal is one of the "children of love" conceived at the sacred wedding. This is confirmed by innumerable tiny pilgrims, each one no bigger than an ant, who approach the crystal, touch it, and run away. I recognize them as the masters of the heart space, the tiny giants mentioned above. I imagine that they approach the crystal in order to renew their attunement with the origin of the philo-sphere. Then I see that the crystal is connected to a sphere of light, swirling with colors and sounds, that envelops the whole island. It is clear to me that this is the philo-sphere of the island of Bled.

Another way in which the philo-sphere emerges in the landscape has to do with the female-male relationships in nature. For an example, I will cite the relationship between the three peaks of Ljubljana's Castle Hill and the river Ljubljanica.

Many years of experience enable me to associate these three "heads" of the castle hill with the three aspects of the human heart system. The hilltop closest to the castle building is where the relationship with the ancestors was celebrated in primal times. Within the structure of Gaia's new heart system, we can perceive a sphere in which we, as embodied humans, can embrace those living as souls in the beyond. This corresponds to the heart center located on the right side of our chest.

The second peak, known as the "redoubt", holds in its depths a jewel similar to the jewel beneath the island of Bled, which we identified as one of the "children of love".

In order to experience the source of the philo-sphere of the third peak, we follow the zig-zag path to the foot of the hill where the broad root system of a tall tree enters the earth. Inside, I experience the presence of a dragon that surrounds and penetrates me in the form of a colorful sphere of light.

The Ljubljanica River approaches the castle hill from the south, embracing it on two sides. The left arm is integrated into the urban landscape. The right arm, which once existed as a river, was later silted up and subsequently reinstated in the seventeenth century as the Gruber drainage canal, with the purpose of draining the Ljubljana Moor.

The Ljubljanica is an unusual river, flowing mostly through a limestone landscape. Since limestone is easily eroded by water, the river disappears six times into underground caves – including the world-famous Postojna Grotto – and is then reborn each time, bringing the experiences of the underworld to the light of the manifest world.

When I stand at the point where the river passes the castle hill, I see that the energy body of the river is rising high and showing it a golden sign in which all its underworld experiences are encoded. The castle hill is covered in countless shimmering water sparks that drip down the slopes of the hill and then get absorbed.

What emerges from the encounter of the river with the hill is a sphere with the quality of the philo-sphere in which both partners are continuously united, and in which I am able to take part as the person who is perceiving.

Venice as a model of the philo-sphere

The cityscape of Venice can also help us to deepen our knowledge of the presence of the philo-sphere in the embodied world of Earth. In my forty years of creative investigation of Venice, I have come to recognize this unique city as a polygon that enables Gaia and her creative entities to create models of the future there with relative ease. Water is present everywhere – and not only in the canals spanned by more than five hundred bridges. The city is built upon countless wooden piles in the water of the lagoon; Venice is a hologram in water embodied in stone (see my book *Venice – Discovering a Hidden Pathway*).

It is no surprise that in the course of the last few years – among other things – a complete model of the renewed philo-sphere of the Earth, with all the aspects mentioned so far, has been fashioned there. Only a few aspects can be outlined here, so as not to flood the whole book with examples from Venice. Above all, we are interested in how the portals of the four elements are incorporated into the composition of the heart fields and heart centers.

The waterway that is the Grand Canal winds its way through the city in an inverted "S" shape and forms the axis around which the central circle of the philo-sphere is built. The two-dimensional reversed "S" shape of the canal is transformed into a circle by two potent power sites on each side. These are the churches of Maria dei Carmini and Maria dei Miracoli which are capable of continuously flipping the mirrored "S" into the regular "S". This creates a sphere that could be compared to the function of the center of the heart in the human being.

Two smaller spheres nourish this heart center at the northern and southern outlets of the Grand Canal. The northern sphere – centered around the now demolished church of Santa Lucia – serves today as a railway station. In relation to the human heart system, this is the elemental heart, addressing the Alpine chain in the city's hinterland. The quality of the elemental heart is best experienced in the nearby Church of the Scalzi, Santa Maria di Nazareth.

At the southern mouth of the Grand Canal, the sphere encloses a spacious water basin, Bacino San Marco. On the banks of the Bacino stand, in a triangle, three of Venice's most important churches, the basilicas of San Giorgio Maggiore, Santa Maria della Salute, and San Marco. I associate this triangle with the "three hearts system" as described in chapter 8, and the system of the third eye is also woven into it. In the atmosphere, various pilgrim paths meet above the Bacino San Marco on which souls from the spiritual world are continually walking. Here, we can perceive a particularly strong emanation of the highest level of the angelic world, to which the seraphim belong, who uphold the philo-sphere of the universe.

The sphere of the Bacino San Marco is nourished and potentized from two sides by the watery dragon power, symbolized by the two waterways, up to four-hundred meters wide, that converge at the Bacino San Marco. The San Marco Canal to the east connects Venice with the dragon power of the Adriatic Sea; the Giudecca Canal to the west connects Venice with the elemental watery power from the Alps.

In chapter 7, I spoke about the role of the dragon force in the human heart system. In regard to these two canals, I will now expand on the interpretations given there. The realm of elemental force, the Earth, recognizes the feminine-masculine polarization as a creative yin-yang tension. In Venice, I experienced the elemental force coming from the East as feminine, as a "dragoness" whose task is to maintain the foundations for the development of life on Earth. The dragon force contained in the western channel, Giudecca, on the other hand, nourishes the foundations of creative processes, including those relating to cultural activity.

The multi-layered synergetic processes at the Bacino San Marco ultimately pour into the Grand Canal, making possible the embodiment of the love impulses in the manifest world, a process that occurs in Venice thanks to the "portals of the four elements" represented by the three churches along the Grand Canal together with the Rialto Bridge. The church of San Vio denotes the portal of the fire element, the church of Santo Stefano the element of air and the associated processes of consciousness. The Rialto Bridge – arching over the Grand Canal – is associated with the element of earth, and the church of San Stae represents the element of water.

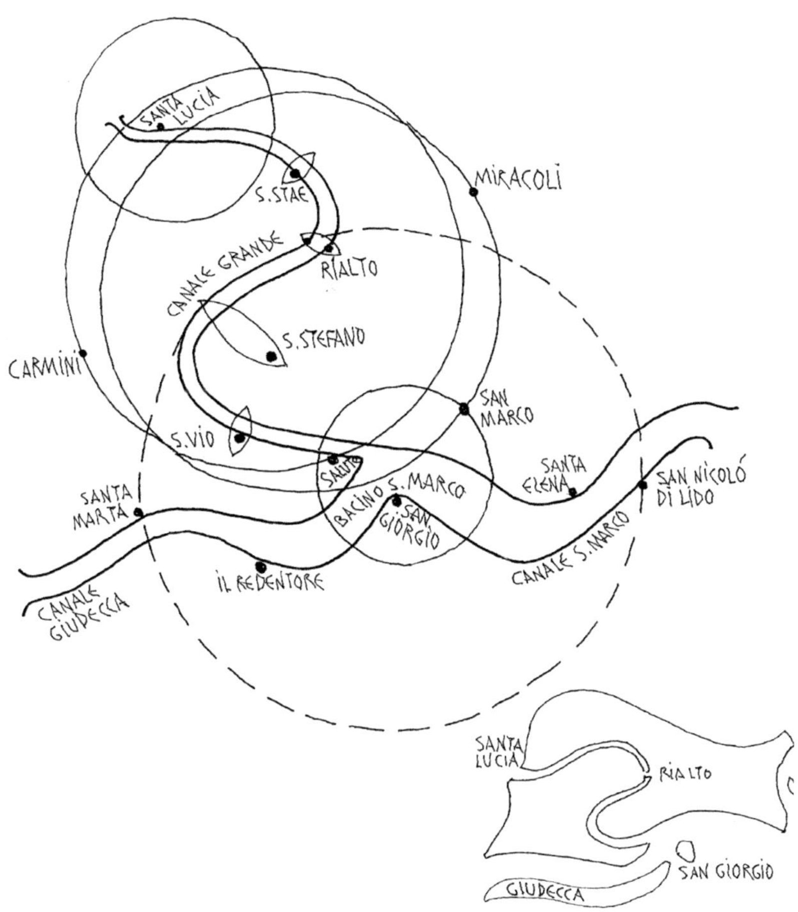

The urban landscape of Venice displays the fish shape – a schematic representation of the philo-sphere of Venice.

11
The philo-sphere of society

To conclude our journey together, I would like to once again raise the question of whether there are love networks in human society that vibrate in a similar way to those in nature and in landscapes.

Unfortunately, the first thing to point out in this context is the destruction in the philo-sphere wrought by the potent electromagnetic and cybernetic networks, especially in urban and industrial areas where wide holes are torn in the life- and love-networks of the landscape. The second cause of the impairment of the philo-sphere is the belligerent actions that periodically break out in the human world. Not a single day goes by without reports of military confrontations in one or another country. There is an archetypal pattern behind this: the ancient Greeks married their goddess of love, Aphrodite, to the god of war, Ares, and the Romans followed by forcing their Venus into a marriage with Mars.

What is the point of talking and writing about love relationships today? Are we as individuals, couples, groups capable of replacing lost love-networks in nature and in the manifest world through our conscious awareness and the activation of the new heart system as described here?

Despite the disturbing factors, the answer to the question is a clear "yes". But this does not mean that humanity has an exclusive position when it comes to the sphere of love; rather, human beings – like all other beings on the various levels of Earth's cosmos – have a very specific task to fulfill within the greater whole. Could it be that we human beings are called to become aware of the heart system in ourselves, which can unite all the different sources of love power in order to transform them into loving deeds on the manifest plane? Have we not been gifted with a heart system vibrating on the various planes of existence, precisely to enable us to consciously maintain the cosmic power of love – in the relationships between the beings of nature, in the elemental world and in interpersonal relationships – and thus to raise this cosmic power of earthly origin to the level that is due to love?

How, then, can we realize the task associated with this gift of a new heart system in a world that is powerfully opposed to acknowledging love as a world-creating force and refuses love its due place on the manifest Earth?

The personal love sphere

Before we – and all beings of the earthly universe – can be embraced by the renewed planetary philo-sphere, we must look for solutions within ourselves. We will have to manifest the personal love sphere within our body and our own life. What do I mean by the personal love sphere?

Earlier I spoke about how Gaia and her co-creators are establishing the offshoots of the new philo-sphere in many landscapes of the Earth. The preparations are under way and finally all the beauty of the love sphere in its wholeness will unfold. Each one of us can collaborate in this process because, as I pointed to in *Universe of the Human Body,* each embodied human being is a micro-landscape. Each of us can help to build the new love sphere of the Earth within the "landscape" of our own multidimensional body, in the same way that a mother offers the embryo the possibility to evolve within her womb. The dream I received on January 15, 2023, sheds light on how to proceed:

> *I have booked a therapy session with a group led by a man who does not tolerate latecomers. My punctuality is an absolutely necessity. However, on my way to the session, just before the therapy is about to begin, I am suddenly detained by a person who wants me to read and sign a paper. Consequently, I am a few minutes late. The group is already practicing, and the teacher stares reproachfully at me. A quick look at the group tells me what the therapy is about. Each person is holding a ball that is wrapped in soft green tissue and is using it to rhythmically touch certain parts of their body. My "ball" is waiting for me on a cabinet close to the entrance. It is not, however, a tissue-wrapped ball, but a big square box.*

The color green stands for the heart chakra in the yogic tradition. Thus, the therapy with the soft green balls appears to symbolize the awakening of the personal love sphere. I do not believe, however, that my square box is simply a punishment for my late arrival. My intuition tells me that it is a sign that we should start by confronting the traumas that block our approach to the personal love sphere. The path to its implementation opens only afterwards.

The paperwork—a necessary formality of the kind our lives are overloaded with on a daily basis—was what caused me to be late. So, what should we do? Don't allow the entanglements of the chaotic outside world to hold you captive. Even if you are faced with a critical situation, surrounded by unavoidable tasks that need to be done, stay in the embrace of your personal love. The feeling of being constantly imbued by the sweet presence of the personal philo-sphere is more important than the mental decision to hold on to it.

What about the contents of that strange box waiting for me at the entrance?

Opening the box, I am confronted with certain sequences of my present and past lives, where I have acted against the patterns of love.

Such traumatic situations are far from being pleasant but are understandable, given that I have spent thousands of years reincarnating into the patriarchal era of suppression, which is more or less hostile towards feminine qualities and powers, and thus also repressing sensitive love relationships. Now the moment is ripe to clear the box.

Should you discover such a "box" in a dream or find yourself confronted with such a trauma-revealing situation, be ready to work on its transmutation immediately. You can lead streams of transforming violet light through that traumatic memory again and again, until it changes into white light. Alternatively, you can catch the traumatic pattern with your hands and press it rhythmically into a homeopathic globule. Give the globule to your elemental helpers and ask them to carry it to the sanctuary of transmutation, which has been newly created in the etheric spaces for this purpose. You can also use the Gaia Touch methods of transformation I have given in my book *Dancing with the Earth Changes.*

How does the dream image of the therapy with the green tissue-wrapped balls translate into the language of logic? I am sure that the new aspects of the human heart system, as described in the previous chapters, hold the key to the self-healing methods unveiled by the dream. The greater part of this treasure – the still dormant possibility of enhancing holistic life forms and more harmonious relationships with nature and our fellow human beings – remains within us. This potential exists as information immersed in the water sphere of our body, and it is this information that needs to be translated into the practical touch of love.

Imagine that the focal points of your heart system are like flower buds. Some buds unfold to blossoms but, instead of producing pollen, a small love globule, as fragile as a soap bubble, emerges out of the flower. Keep this love bubble within the corresponding spaces of your body to gradually strengthen and build up your personal love sphere. Afterwards, allow the philo-sphere bubble to glide into your environment and then further into the world to partake in the process of rebuilding the love sphere of the Earth.

As we experience inwardly the personal sources of love and the focal points of the heart system, we will gradually embody and ground the potential of the philo-sphere that resides in the water body of the human being. This process is not just our own individual inner experience, it also shows itself outwardly in daily life, opening up new possibilities for us. Then we are able to learn to master our own conflicts and unfortunate situations in a creative and peaceful way. Not only will we behave more lovingly towards our fellow human beings, but we will also open up towards our own elemental nature.

Geoculture - Gaia Culture

The only credible way towards rebuilding the philo-sphere of society that I can see is for this to be incorporated into the processes of transformation of the Earth – which I addressed at the beginning of this book. I use the term "Earth transformation" to describe a partially invisible process, the phenomena of which I have been observing since late autumn 1997. This involves the Earth – as a planet permeated with elemental consciousness – gradually and imperceptibly but consciously changing her being in the subtle areas of her planetary body, to give rise to a multidimensional Earth space that does not erase the existence of three-dimensional reality with which we are familiar but incorporates it into a new and broader spatial composition.

Parallel to this, a process of human transformation is taking place. The traumas and blockages rooted in the epochs when humankind separated from Gaia and the beings of the earthly universe are now surfacing on the personal and collective level to be gradually redeemed. Countless difficulties remain to be faced. Along with the new Earth, a new culture is emerging, which I call Gaia Culture.

May the book you hold in your hands and the attention that you invest as a reader, help Gaia Culture to swiftly manifest the renewal of the philo-sphere on Earth.

12

Exercises and imaginations

Welcome to the exercises! I wish you success and precious experiences. My exercises usually combine imaginations with certain minimal physical activities. This creates a synergy that opens the doors of perception. I would like to clarify that imaginations are not visualizations, that is, they are not mental projections. Imagining means imbuing the created images with the corresponding feelings. Sometimes it takes some practice to coordinate the physical movement, which is often also imaginative, with the congruent feeling and image.

Trees and plants

1. Experiencing the inner life of a tree

- Imagine: A tree is behind your back—if you want, you can imagine a tree you know, but that is not necessary.
- Now take a few steps backwards as if you were going through the trunk of the tree. After going through the inside of the tree and finally stepping out of the tree, how does it feel?
- You can also do the same exercise with an actual tree. Stand a few steps in front of the tree and turn your back to it. Now take a few steps backwards and walk through the tree (imaginatively, of course!). What do you feel and sense after you have stepped out of the tree?

2. Developing a loving relationship with a tree

- Choose an older solitary tree and stand with your back to the trunk. Make sure that you are standing within the perimeter of the crown. (The roots of a tree extend into the Earth as far as the width of the crown.)
- Now imagine that the tree touches your head with the tip of a branch and the roots touch the soles of your feet.

- Further, imagine and feel how you bring the touch of the root up to your heart space and the touch of the branch tip down to your heart, so that both meet in your heart center. Take time to feel and enjoy this loving encounter within yourself.

3. Experiencing the love relationships between trees

- Go into a nearby wood or forest and stand among the trees.
- Imagine white threads stretching from the center of your heart to the trees around you. Imagine these threads attached to the tree trunks at a height above your head.
- Then bend your knees a little, so that your buttocks are a little closer to the ground, and do a little jump upwards. Don't worry, the trees themselves will lift you up to the height where they maintain their love fields.
- Close your eyes at this moment to feel the love force-field of the forest—or keep your eyes open if you prefer. In any case, enjoy the Anwa of the forest until you land on the ground again.
- You can repeat the exercise until you get the coordination right between your imagination, your body movement, and the beings of the forest.

4. Experiencing the love scent of flowers

- Approach the flower with your face. Look at it lovingly for a few moments.
- Then imagine you are a bee and glide inside the flower—not to get honey, but to experience its interior.
- While there, move and spin around, or even somersault, to enjoy as much of the love scent as possible.
- Repeat this imagination with another flower to feel the difference between different types of flowers—and be grateful for the experience.

5. Experiencing the love relationships between plants

- Sit comfortably among the plants in a garden.
- To experience the Anwa of the small plants, you must first make yourself small. Your imagination has the ability to reduce your size to the scale of the plants you want to experience from within.

- Now you can walk among the plants as if you were among trees in a forest.
- At a certain moment, take your small self into your heart center to perceive the love relationships between the plants that is stored in your memory. Then you can continue your walk among the plants.

Stones, rocks, and mountains

1. *Experiencing the stone as consciousness*

- Choose the stone you want to communicate with.
- Stand in front of the stone and move around the stone in your imagination to touch it at its back.
- Now both the stone and you are at the same level of consciousness.
- Simply enter the sphere of the stone and explore its expanses now.
- Come back to your everyday consciousness and give thanks.

2. *Experiencing the stone in relationship to the heart of Gaia*

- You are standing in front of a stone.
- Hold your hands at the level of your elemental heart (at the lower tip of the sternum) with the palms facing upwards horizontally in front of you.
- Bring your hands a little forward and imagine that you are now holding your hands underneath the stone.
- In your imagination, lift the stone a little.
- Once you have lifted the stone, you can experience its relationship to the Earth's core or explore its inner life.
- Replace the stone on the ground and draw your hands back to your body.

This exercise, especially with heavy stones or rocks, is best done in a group standing around the stone. One person should give the signal with the word "Now" so that everyone can start the action at the same time. A similar signal should be given when the rock needs to be returned to its place on the ground. Afterwards, you can share your experiences.

3. *Embracing mountains, stones, and crystals*

- While standing facing a mountain, hold up both hands with the palms vertically facing each other, their clearance corresponding to the breadth of the mountain as observed by your eyes.
- Then make a gesture as if you want to hug the mountain by bringing your hands around the mountain until the two middle fingers touch (at the back of the mountain).
- Now bring this hugging gesture (and with it the mountain) closer to the center of your heart. But leave enough space for the mountain to breathe.
- Now begin to sense the loving relationship between the two of you.
- Then open your hands so that the mountain can return to its place.

The same exercise can also be done with stones and crystals. Before the embracing, make sure that you adjust the distance between your hands to the width of the stone or crystal as registered by your eyes.

The personal elemental being

1

- Imagine that there is a shallow lake in the bowl formed by your hips and pelvic area.
- Drops of water fall rhythmically and continuously from the tip of your sternum into the lake, creating ring-shaped waves.
- Now imagine that these create a wave-like resonance with the different levels of your body.
- Begin to perceive and sense yourself as an elemental being.
- Welcome this.

2

- Sit down and imagine that there is a bead of light in each of your knees.
- These two beads travel through your body on different paths without meeting each other.
- In the middle of your heart space, they collide. A spark of light is created.
- Become one with this spark of light to experience and know your elemental master.

The unified love theory of humanity

1

- Remember someone you love who has passed away, or one whom you suspect has a message for you.
- Just now, only the person's face is important. Expand his or her face until it fills the whole room in front of you.
- Now stand up. Step toward the face until you merge with the face.
- Feel the presence of that soul and develop a silent conversation with that soul.

2

- Imagine a white cylinder resting vertically on your shoulders that is just a little higher than your hands raised above your head.
- Now move your hands carefully into the cylinder as far as you can.
- Move your fingers in the cylinder, following the language of your soul, until you feel contact with the sphere of souls.
- Now move your hands wider apart so that the cylinder dissolves. While keeping your hands outstretched, connect with your heart level.
- Feel with your fingers that the sphere of the spiritual world exists around you, but on a different vibrational level.

The dragon heart

- Sit on a chair so that your thighs are straight and bend your head down.
- Imagine that a force from within the Earth is pushing against your heels, lifting your feet until they touch your forehead (the movement is imaginative!).
- Now bring your hands around your feet and embrace them until your middle fingers touch each other.
- Then dissolve the embracing gesture and bring your hands to your heart.
- In that moment, feel the power and the loving wisdom of the dragon within you.

The sphere of love – the philo-sphere

- In your imagination, choose a place you know that is shell-like in shape or is in some way imbued with the feminine quality.
- Breathe together with the place, imagining that when you breathe in, the breath is drawn up from the center of the Earth (from the heart of Gaia) to its surface.
- Exhaling, imagine that small, fine beads, like soap bubbles, are exhaled. They shimmer in rainbow colors and gradually fill the whole room.
- Stand up and move around in the space between the "bubbles" for a while to experience the quality of the philo-sphere.

The system of the three hearts

Gaia Touch Exercise with the "Three Hearts"

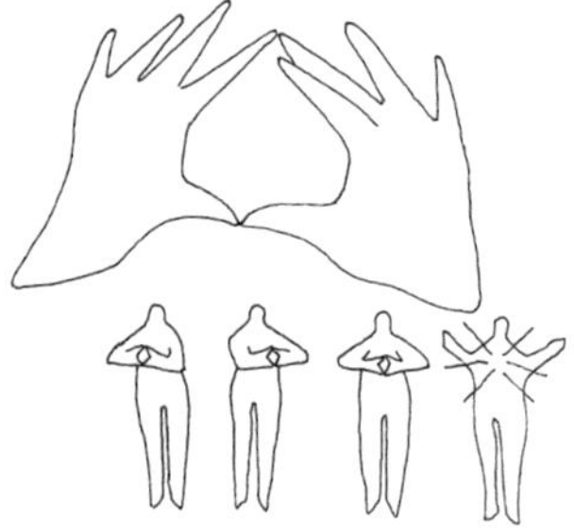

- Form a mandorla with your hands in front of your heart center, using the middle finger of one hand and the index finger of the other hand, as well as both thumbs (see the drawing above).
- Move the mandorla first to the left to connect with your heart muscle, then to the right to touch the fractal of the common heart of humanity.
- When moving your hands to the left, turn your head slightly to the right; when moving them to the right, turn your head to the left. This indicates that the movement is not only in front but also behind the back.
- Bring your hands back to your heart center; your head facing forward.
- Now open your hands wide and become aware of your heart power.

The heart space

- To connect with the heart center behind the back, take five steps backwards and—without pausing—three steps forwards again. Repeat this rhythmic sequence of steps several times. It is best to do this exercise first physically a few times and then imaginatively for a while, visualizing that you are stepping into your back space.
- As you take more steps backwards than forwards each time, after a while you will find the treasure chamber of your heart, where the archetypes of the philo-sphere reside. Feel their presence.
- Next, to experience the quality of the heart center in front of the chest take five steps forward and three steps back a few times. As you do it imaginatively, visualize yourself stepping into the space in front of you.
- Now you can experience your heart center pulsating exactly midway between the two partial centers in the middle of your chest.

The faery heart

- Sit on a chair so that your thighs are straight. Imagine that your second self is standing on your knees. As your second self is smaller than you, you can look into each other's eyes. Connect with your essence through eye contact.
- Then let your second self rise higher until it stands on your shoulders and looks into the space behind your back.
- What you now see in front of you from the perspective of your second self (in your back space) is a lake covered with a very thin layer of ice. Make yourself extremely light and walk across this layer of ice to the other side of the lake.
- You now stand in front of a city built of ethereal material that looks as if it were white marble.
- Go into the city and ask the inhabitants for the key that will allow you to experience your own faerylike realm.
- Return the same way with the key in your hand to resonate with the faery aspect within yourself.

The animal world

- Imagine holding a young doe on your knees. Feel her presence.
- Then feel her love field, with which she touches your heart area.
- Now allow for certain qualities of your heart system to flow into the love field that is building between you.
- Listen for the response of her love field.
- Give thanks to the doe and get up to leave her to its natural habitat again.

A kinesiogram to call elemental guardian angels to your aid

I suggest a kinesiogram ("a sign with motive power") for summoning the help of the elemental guardian angels (see p. 80). Like cosmograms, these are a form of universal language that I developed in the 1980s.

The drawing below shows the shape of the kinesiogram for protection. The "X" is for defense and the four corners represent the four heart sources revealed in this book. They are focused in the center, in the heart center, so that protection is not established violently, but through the cooperation of all five centers of the new heart system.

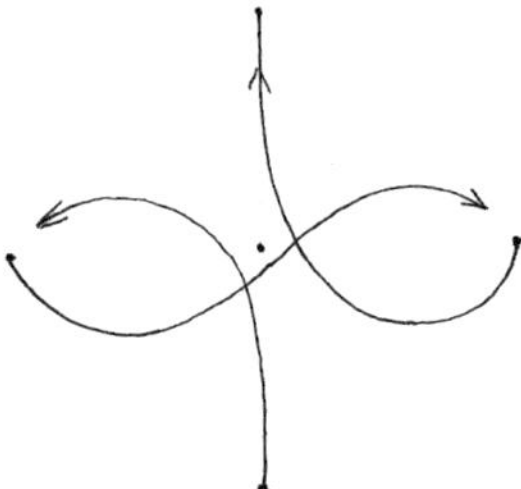

- With all five fingertips of one hand drawn together in a point, describe the kinesiogram in the space in front of you with an outstretched arm.
- Start in one of the four corners of the kinesiogram and draw the shape several times without interruption and in a solemn attitude.
- Afterwards you can feel that the protection does not come from outside, but from within your heart.

A kinesiogram to connect with the philo-sphere

See the instructions for kinesiograms in the previous exercise. In this case, three "dots" are added. You create a dot by stopping delineating for a split second, followed by brief pointing forward and then immediately continuing with the line. Dots are important for lodging the sign in the universal memory.

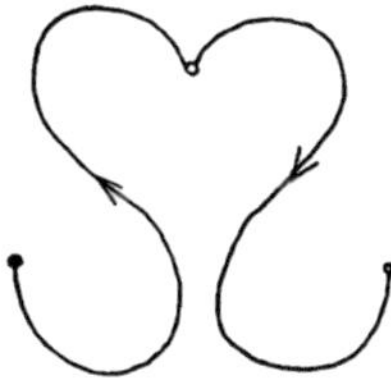

- The kinesiogram is made up of two "S" shapes, one positioned correctly and the second inverted. In between are the three dots. Both "S" shapes refer to the form of the Grand Canal in Venice as described in chapter 10.
- You can draw the sign several times in succession, once from left to right and then from right to left. Start with the left or the right dot and don't forget the dot in between.

13

Renewing the love sphere of the Earth

The last two chapters have showed that in order to restore the Earth's philo-sphere we must first of all reconnect with our own human essence and also work consistently to connect with our environment. But several unexpected dreams I received during the transition from the year 2022 to 2023 revealed that restoring the love sphere cannot succeed without the cooperation of the primary creative system of the Earth and the universe. What do I mean by this primary creative system? Part of the answer can be found in the dream that I had during the first night of 2023:

I have brought my child to music school. While waiting in the school's front yard until the lesson is finished, I look around the yard, which is bereft of anything interesting. The rectangular school building is tall, grey, and unfriendly, so I decide to go around the corner to take a look at the back yard. This has the exact same dimensions as the front yard. Also, some pieces of rubbish are lying on the ground, but nothing of great interest.

Then I notice that beyond the back yard is a third yard of the same size as the previous two. But this one is completely filled up with old building materials and tools. There are large pieces of scaffolding, a huge amount of paneling units, a crane, etc. I realize that they are left from building the music school decades ago, and should have long ago been disposed of.

The front yard can be likened to the manifest world that extends in front of our body and is perceivable through our five physical senses. The yard behind the building – the space behind our back, so to say – represents the causal extension of existence with its archetypal patterns, the living space of the elemental beings who form and transform the manifested face of life (remember the story of "Rapunzel" from chapter 2 with the miracle garden located at the back of the house). The dream also reveals to me a further – hitherto unknown – causal dimension behind the familiar causal world, where the tools and forces needed for building and transforming the space of reality embodied in matter are stored.

To be honest, the discovery of a new causal system surprised me. I had been convinced that the causal world, as a unified system, was entirely responsible for the manifestations of the physical world, including plants, minerals, animals, elemental beings, landscapes, and people. Now I need to accept the existence of a deeper level of the causal world that seems to play a decisive role in the process of embodying and building up the love sphere in daily life. Why else would there be such a quantity of building materials heaped up in my dream? Quite obviously, the building materials stored there are useless when it comes to embodying love relationships, yet they tell us that this area of the causal world is related to creative processes. I am convinced that beneath all the building materials are to be found the knowledge capable of renewing the extremely sensitive membrane of the philo-sphere, as well as the corresponding creative beings.

Transposing this realm to the human body, this primary creative power originates in the depths of the abdominal cavity. This is where I perceive the focus of the feminine aspect of the dragon power (which I call the "white dragoness"). I know her as the source of the philo-sphere that has been within us since the epoch when the biosphere and conscience of the human body were not yet separated from the love sphere of the Earth.

Let us now remember the "dragon tongue" connected to the dragon powers in the human heart system that I addressed in chapter 7: "Where can I find in the human heart muscle the mighty heart power of the dragons, which after all should be capable of amplifying a thousand times over the power of love that flows from the human heart? Why is the love radiating from human hearts so weak that we have to watch powerlessly as wars rage mercilessly around us?"

As we approach the end of our journey, I am now able offer a more comprehensive answer to the question: What role does the dragon tongue play in relation to the heart system of the Earth and its beings?

The dragon tongue is a symbol of the deepest causal level of existence that can guide love impulses on their way to embodiment in the manifest dimension of the world. If the nuclear power of awakened human hearts and the wisdom of love flowing from the Earth's philo-sphere were to freely suffuse our physical reality, we would be able to breathe with more than just one third of our lung capacity. And instead of being powerless in the face of the raging wars, we would be capable of recreating new and happy relationships between all beings existing on all the levels of the Earth's manifest creation. So why is this not yet possible?

The above dream offers a partial answer to this question. The causal system of the dragon tongue, which is capable of transporting the almost limitless love power to the embodied level of creation, is totally blocked by the "building implements" that were only appropriate for making manifest the old world governed by the rational constrictions and patriarchal appetites of modern civilization. Countless scientific research projects at odds with the wholeness of the earthly universe have opened the gates for a flood of even more destructive technologies and behaviors that aim to manipulate any and every possible aspect of the physical world. Perhaps the most sacred chapter in the evolution of Earth is the embodiment in matter (a potential sanctuary for love relationships on the planet), and this has been turned into a battlefield for commercial and political interests over centuries.

It is hard to believe the primary creative system of the Earth and the universe is subjected to such a complete occupation. This is ridiculous because its roots reach down to the deepest causal level, almost to the core of Divinity, to the most protected level of creation. To express it poetically, it is the point of eternity, where no difference exists between the creative input of the elemental realms on one side and the angelic realms on the other. Both are one. Yet it is not just the point of eternity, but also an all-embracing causal system behind the known causal system that is responsible for the existence and non-existence of all that is, including the creation of matter on Earth and in the universe.

At the beginning of the chapter, I called this realm "the primary creative system of the Earth and the universe". If for a moment I dare to eliminate from this causal field all the building implements that I saw in my dream, I can recognize that the source of this primary creative system is the heart of Gaia, where it gets imbued with the vision and the creative wisdom of the Mother of Life. Simultaneously, I can perceive an inflow from a complementary level, from the core of the universe. I see drops of cosmic inspiration rhythmically falling upon the golden plate of the earthly causal system. I experience both processes as united, as a oneness capable of renewing the Earth's philo-sphere in accordance with the current cosmic cycles.

For the decades and the centuries to come, we must expect to witness difficult upheavals on Earth both in nature and in human society, a profound cleansing and retuning of the alienated layers of the causal and manifest levels of existence. Only then will all the obstacles be removed and the way be clear for the primary creative powers of the Earth and the cosmos (which are actual beings) to transform the embodied worlds and restore the Love Sphere of Earth.

Manifesto of the Free Earth

I wrote this Manifesto of the Free Earth *with charcoal upon a 36-foot high wall at the Švicarija Culture and Art Center in Ljubljana, capital of my country Slovenia, in December 2022.*

Mother, Mother, is it true that "climate change" will turn green meadows into wastelands and dry up the clear rivers and streams?

Mother, Mother, is it true that masses of climate refugees will flood Europe and famine will plague human populations between the South and the North?

Mother, Mother, is it true that the Sun will shine so brightly that the ladybirds will fly away and people will go to the afterlife in huge waves?

Mother, Mother, is the Earth really a dead thing, incapable of helping animals, plants, people, landscapes, and dolphins in dire need?

The Earth is not a dead thing made up of hard rocks, clothed only in a thin layer of life tissue. The Earth is first and foremost an elemental consciousness.

The Earth as a conscious being knows that the cosmic cycle has turned, that the time of human autocracy inflated by the will to power and authority has come to an end.

The Earth as a co-creator in the revelation of a new round of cosmic evolution knows that an age of interplay of opposites is coming.

The Earth is a living being made up of countless tiny suns, which hold a memory from eternity to the end of eternity.

In order to prevent the disintegration of the fabric of life, the Earth has raised the energetic pulse of its worlds and their beings to a new level of existence.

In order to provide enough space for all beings, visible and invisible, to evolve, the Earth is opening the door to spaces that are currently unknown to us.

Split into different dimensions, the Earth is able to accommodate all beings determined to preserve and love the Earth as a place of creative coexistence.

At the same time, the Earth closes the door to forces and powers that are not dedicated to life and are not ready to exist and act in harmony with the essence of being.

The Earth, as the creator of the embodied world, opens the gates of the Water element, leading into the halls of health and the landscapes of healing.

The Earth, as the mother of embodied creation, opens the gates of the Earth element, leading to the causal worlds of being where ideas take form.

The Earth, as the creator of reality, opens the gates of the Fire element, leading to truth as the simple truth of life.

The Earth, as the mother of the world of revelation, opens the gates of the Air element, leading to the insight of what is the meaning of existence and creation on Earth.

Mother, Mother, is it true that the landscapes of the Earth are inhabited by innumerable elemental beings invisible to us, the guardians of life in nature?

Mother, Mother, is it true that the dead dwell not far from us as invisible companions and guardians of the incarnate human race?

Mother, Mother, is it true that the dragons sustain and renew the core force of life that cannot be erased, suppressed, or permanently enslaved?

Mother, Mother, is the Earth really a living expression of infinite love, capable of realizing a paradise-like value of existence if we decide to follow her inspiration?

Books referenced in the text

David Spangler *Engaging with the Sidhe,* Lorian Press, USA, 2017

Ana Pogačnik *Being Human in the Now,* www.menschseinimjetzt.de, 2022

Marko Pogačnik *Christ Power and Earth Wisdom,* Clairview Books, 2020

Creating Gaia Culture, Clairview Books, 2022

Dancing with the Earth Changes, Lindisfarne Books, 2021

Nature Spirits & Elemental Beings, Findhorn Press, 2010

Universe of the Human Body, Lindisfarne Books 2016

Venice–Discovering a Hidden Pathway, with photographs by Bojan Brecelj, Lindisfarne Bools, 2008

About the author

Marko Pogačnik (b. 1944) lives with his wife and collaborator Marika in Šempas, Slovenia. In the 1960s Marko worked as a conceptual and land artist in the OHO group, a Slovene artist collective that was the first "radical urban-ideological" artistic appearance in Slovene modern art and a significant movement in the context of Slovene national culture, Yugoslavian socialist culture, and international youth culture. Marko later developed lithopuncture, a method of Earth healing using cosmograms carved on stone pillars.

Since 2005, Marko has built Geopuncture stone circles worldwide, together with an international team of colleagues. For over two decades he has been focusing on collaborating with the Earth-changing process, developing Gaia Touch body exercises and the vision of a Geoculture, which he calls Gaia Culture. In 2016, he was appointed as Artist for Peace and UNO Goodwill Ambassador by the Secretary General of UNESCO.

Marko's books in English include, among others: *Grimm's Fairy Tales Decoded* (2025), *Creating Gaia Culture* (2022), *Dancing with the Earth Changes* (2021), *Christ Power and Earth Wisdom* (2020), *Universe of the Human body* (2016), *Gaia's Quantum Leap* (2011), *Nature Spirits & Elemental Beings* (2010), *Venice: Discovering a Hidden Pathway* (2008), *Sacred Geography* (2007), and *Turned Upside Down* (2004).

Visit: www.markopogacnik.com